# My Heart is a Stone
# That Bleeds

# My Heart is a Stone That Bleeds

### Karl P. Whitehead

Writer's Showcase
San Jose  New York  Lincoln  Shanghai

# My Heart is a Stone
# That Bleeds

Writer's Showcase
an imprint of iUniverse, Inc.

For information address:
iUniverse, Inc.
5220 S. 16th St., Suite 200
Lincoln, NE 68512
www.iuniverse.com

**Library of Congress Registration:** TXu1010768

ISBN: 0-595-24165-4

Printed in the United States of America

This book is dedicated to my wife Kathie who stands by me everyday in everyway. Thank you Kathie, I love you. You truly are my special angel.

*"Great spirits have always encountered violent opposition from mediocre minds."*
—Albert Einstein

# *Contents*

## *Part III*

# Preface

The alcoholic legacy to a non drinking child of an alcoholic parent is sometimes hard to recognize and accept. It may also be a prominent attribute. People suffering from the legacy are often chronically depressed, dishonest, confused, and prone to being abused and to abuse others. They are often predisposed to alcoholism and denial and will either play the victim or create victims by abusing them. Living in a house where the alcoholic legacy is multi generational guarantees some form of distress associated with the ACAP (adult children of alcoholics) syndrome will be passed down. Often the symptoms appear only as an indefinable, pervasive anxiety and fear because painful memories are often blocked, denied or edited in some fashion.

Memory is often the hardest part of the human experience to quantify. What we remember is often tainted by age, distance, emotion and denial. One person will sometimes not remember an incident as another does decades later. Emotions are tied to this idea. What one person feels decades later is not always what another feels even when they experience the same ordeal. In the course of reading this book there may be those who say they didn't remember a particular incident that way. They may claim the description deletes certain data or embellishes the story in some way. They may claim it didn't happen at all. To the best of my recollection the words and stories herein are true and complete. Although many incidents have been excluded because of their repetitious and voluminous nature, the remaining stories are a comprehensive representation of my childhood.

The deletion of the names and ages of family members was a deliberate act to protect the privacy of those who do not support my cathartic writing as a necessary part of my emotional recovery. Every attempt was made to protect their right to privacy while I exercise my right to free speech. The only way to protect them further is not to tell the story all. Additionally, I refuse to lie about what happened or fictionalize any part of it. To those who are offended with the words herein I apologize. And add this suggestion; if you don't agree with what I have to say, write your own book. This is my story and I will stand by it and my right to tell it. For those who feel this story is a sad example of victimization, I would respond by saying the intent of the work is to purge all aspects of the alcoholic legacy. I am attempting to shed the legacy and the victim identity by documenting the abuse and publishing it.

The level of abuse suffered at the hands of an alcoholic parent is often underestimated. The experiences of each child differ as well. If the children are spread out over a span of nearly twenty years the experiences with the parent in question will be in some cases totally different. Therefore, one cannot always testify to the abuse of another. One also cannot deny the abuse of another. Mental and emotional scars will take different forms and each child will have his own baggage to either carry through life, dump along the way or resolve. The quality of each person's passage is ultimately up to that individual alone manifested in the choices they will make or fail to make. What are your choices?

*My Heart is a Stone That Bleeds* is the culmination of many years of seeking resolution to some difficult personal issues. I did not endeavor to do this joyfully and in fact the process of finishing this task was at times more painful than I care to write about. I wrote this book to organize my feelings about a painful and confusing past and then to purge the emotion that has come to define me. My subsequent hope is that the words herein will offer comfort and solace to those who have suffered in the same way.

# Acknowledgements

To Gail Stephens Ph.D. I owe a debt of gratitude I can never repay. Her focus and diligence in working with me in my emotional recovery has been remarkable and honorable. Her insight and vision into the Post Traumatic Stress Disorder was gifted from a higher source than education. Gail is truly a credit to her profession and to merely thank her for helping me would never be enough.

Special thanks to fellow author and long time friend Robert Daras Tatam for his overview and direction of this work. His continued work in literature over these many years has been an inspiration to me as I grow into my own writing shoes. Always honest at the risk of being harsh, Bob's knowledge of books and their impact on society is unique and his help to me in this regard immeasurable.

I would like to extend a very special recognition to Roberta Polumbo and Ken Hogarty who as college professors taught me to write and inspired me to write well. Each of these English teachers had a special impact on me, my writing ability and style. Their continued dedication to education and literature of all types is of benefit to all who know them. Special thanks to both of you for your help over these many years.

I offer a special thank you to Holy Names College in Oakland, its faculty and staff for giving me the financial support and opportunity to start my formal education and discover my love of writing.

Last but not least I thank St. Mary's College in Moraga for the opportunity to complete my education, for the polish on my writing style and for the honors they bestowed me.

Thank you all so very much.

# PART I

# My Heart is a Stone That Bleeds

Time is rigid and unforgiving. The hours of inner turmoil often turn to days of non productive despair as I try to locate the source of my undefined anxiety. Panic attacks and fear overwhelm me at times for no reason at all. Denial makes time feel more fluid and less painful. Denial is the friend of all who suffer through relationships of any kind where alcohol use brings emotional abuse, uncertainty and destabilized trust. The shadow over me darkened the path from my childhood through a history of shattered dreams. A long time has past since then but the nightmares continue. There is no escape from what I have become. I am an adult child of an alcoholic parent.

Now is always better than before. However, the present sometimes offers the opportunity for the past to come forth and haunt me, even as I write this. Such is the legacy of the multi generation alcoholic experience. Even though I am removed from the substance and those who would abuse me, I can never really escape the legacy. The legacy defines me even though I have never been an alcoholic myself. I am the son of an alcoholic parent who was the son of alcoholic parents. I have made many sacrifices to break the legacy. At times I lack the vision needed for such an endeavor but I stumble on.

I just passed through another Christmas without any calls from my immediate family. I have no contact with anyone other than one of my sisters. The seeds for this inevitable report have been present for a long time. Growing up in an alcoholic household breeds contempt from those who would enable the drunk against those who would rebel. I was one who rebelled. It was neither a role I chose nor relished. I did it for survival. I believe I am hated for it. A harsh conclusion I reached when no one would talk to me anymore.

The perception of reality for a battered child is at best an incongruent series of events and recollections. These events and recollections are intensified or diminished as the prorated amount of pain is associated with them. One child's memory of an incident is, over time, not going to be exactly what another child remembers even if they experience the same incident. I do not remember my childhood as my siblings would and I will probably not remember their experiences the way they do.

Such is the way growing up in the alcoholic family. The unpredictable nature of alcoholism nurtures a lifestyle where everyone learns to lie to protect themselves. As children we learned to develop a fantasy world tailor made to attenuate the indiscriminate onslaught of pain and sometimes terror. Each child lives in his own dream world to escape the harsh realities thrust upon them. In a volatile and sometimes violent home life, children are often the punching bags for the drunk who is out of control. In this reality any given situation will create a dominant figure, a victim, an excuse or a lie, and the perpetual legacies of denial and abuse. This is a confusing ordeal for adults and devastating for normal mental and emotional development in children. A classic model of the dysfunctional family is created. It becomes a perpetual boxing match in which no one emerges as the winner.

In this situation more emotional children will sometimes spin windmills into demons as Don Quixote did, while others see only windmills. Some more battered children see nothing at all. In years past, my feelings surrounding this subject were often confused and disconnected. The pervasive undefined anxiety is terrible emotional place to exist. Still I haven't lost all hope of pushing past this angry place where many adult children of alcoholics dwell in later life. Although I am not an alcoholic, I have been no stranger to anger and my own emotional abuse of others. I believe I am some years past all that now. Only a shadow of the angry man still lives inside me. The angry man role is a product of abuse and is part of the enduring legacy of alcoholism past from generation to generation. In spite of this some clarity now shines through for me. My path through this emotional maze has been narrow and full of danger. I very often shrink from the task of emotional recovery, even the thought of it. Sometimes there is no where to hide. As a child I escaped by creating illusions of fantasy. Projecting myself into movies and television shows of the time I imagined I was just another character living a normal uneventful life save for the minor crisis's arising during each film or episode. I never saw anything on television that resembled what went on at home. When I began to imagine home wasn't real, the sting of the belt brought me out of my daydreams and I was made to feel stupid and insignificant.

Escapist illusion of my situation brought me, the abused child, to deny my factually painful reality for most of my childhood. However, as an adult I somehow retain many of the facts with total recall unembellished by the nightmarish tone of my recollections. I hope someday to break the cycle of self deprecation handed down through generations of alcoholism and create a new and enduring legacy for myself. I seek a legacy that prohibits denial and provides for truth to prevail and feelings from the heart to flourish. For me, a break in the continuity of family was a necessary first step for this process. For most people in my situation the end of family contact can come after an incident or after a long period or history of abuse.

In my case the end of contact came a few months after my mother died very suddenly from complications of diabetes. My father, the drinker in this case, had died fifteen years before. The family unit perched itself on a tenuous equilibrium for many years after my father's death from cancer coming together only on the holidays and only to visit my mother. When she died the family unit fell apart. It actually divided itself into two factions. There were the ones who questioned the status quo and the ones who claimed to know all the answers.

As a terrible coincidence, my mother died nearly one month to the day before my wedding to Kathie. We decided to proceed with the wedding as I knew my mother would have wished for it. Her death was unexpected but we later found she had been preparing her part early on. For example, she had already wrapped our wedding presents. Birthday cards for the next few months of family birthdays were already signed and in their envelopes. Only my wife and I were astonished by this. During this time certain family members became distracted by the material things that might improve their respective conditions. Things like a non existent life insurance policy and other phantom treasures buried somewhere in her house. However, the house was locked by the executor and nothing was supposed to be removed until some sort of inventory was taken. However, no inventory was taken and the rooms full of items began to disappear anyway. With so much planning and preparation to do on our wedding, I didn't notice things were happening behind my back. After all, I should be able to trust my family in such a time of grief, right? Wrong.

The wedding day came and we were elated to finally be married. It was a great day and people, even estranged family members, genuinely seemed to have a good time. It would come to be the last time my dwindling family was all together in one place. Kathie and I were married outside in a garden with our friends playing music and singing. Friends and family came from many states and as far away as Norway. We had the reception at the restaurant on the property. There were a few foibles but everything generally went well. It was a great relief to me to have such a positive distraction. As the afternoon went on we both felt a sense of relief and joy. Soon we left on our honeymoon. A week at the coast in a rented house, our cocker spaniel safely off at camp (the kennel). We worried about little and I found myself "present" for the whole week.

Unknown to us while we were gone, some family members went into my mother's house and began to load boxes into a car and speed off after every foray into the structure. I know this because there were several messages from the neighbor on our answering service questioning who was doing this. The neighbor thought, as I did, no one was to take anything from the house. It turned out other family members were aware of this activity. One sister, stunned with grief, could do little to stop the actions because she lived in another state and had left soon after the wedding. It seems there was no authoritative direction or oversight in the early disposition of my mother's belongings. The project quickly got out of control.

The executor had heard my initial warnings this might happen and was apparently unaware of the removal of many valuable collectable items. He had asked me at the moment we were leaving the wedding if there was anything in particular that I wanted from the house. Not knowing what was in the house and confronted as we left for our honeymoon, I was somewhat at a loss to produce a list. I foolishly trusted everyone might watch out for me. For example, I didn't know all my classic comic books would vanish into thin air. They were mine and everyone knew it, still no one saw anything. The story is the same for many other items belonging to me. Basically, this is a continuation of the denial produced by the alcoholic legacy. Although the executor may be exposed to some blame in this, overall I believe he did a great job in the disposition of my mother's assets. In fact he eventually handled the situation with remarkable focus considering what and who he had to work with. I couldn't have done it.

In spite of this, many pieces of furniture and other valuable collectibles went missing. When I questioned each member of the family the answer was the same; no one knew what had happened to them. The excuses and lies were incredible and intolerable. At one point I dropped by my mother's house to find several people I had never met rummaging through her things. When I asked a brother who they were he responded by saying they were friends or family of his wife who were good at "helping". Not one of them acknowledged my presence with a single hello and treated me as if I were totally invisible while they picked through my mother's things and put them in bags for themselves. I was however, asked to bring my truck over to remove the ever growing pile of garbage in the yard. Should I feel good that I was finally needed for something? I knew I was being had. I just didn't know when or how it would all come to a head.

There were numerous incidents and conflicts during this time. The end came finally when the pictures of me as a child disappeared. There had been an agreement between the executor and the siblings. As my mother's house was cleared, all photographs and their frames were to be put in a box for later distribution. One day I realized the box had vanished. Upon inquiry, everyone again claimed no knowledge of its whereabouts. During a time when I was alone in the house on garbage duty I searched the numerous garbage bags and found several photographs of me, frames gone, and pictures torn into pieces. My rage was immeasurable. The most deliberate insult of my adult life would shape my future actions forever. How could anyone do such a thing? If not for the fact that I had collected a few pictures of me as a child over the years, the record of my past would have been all but destroyed in these most disgusting of passive aggressive actions. I decided then and there I would no longer associate myself with this group of people previously known as my family.

This incident stands as an example of the long history of abuse that I have endured as a child of an alcoholic parent. The classic enabling roles are taken, not just by the non drinking parent but, by some of the children as well. When the abuser died, the role passed to another and the alcoholic legacy of abuse and denial continued into yet another generation. The obvious lies and theft of my past are not the worst I have suffered in this family. This last of incidents was however, the straw that broke the camel's back. This form of passive aggression is a revolting result of the alcoholic legacy. I informed the executor to tell everyone taking the valuables that they must also take the garbage as well. I didn't want anything more except my share of the house. With rage and disgust I told him to sell the house and send me a check. I've had enough. When I said no to abuse I said goodbye to my family. I was 43 years old at the time this happened. My eventual emotional recovery was a long time overdue. Some events leading to and during this process are chronicled here.

# *Feelings That Hurt*

As an abused child I learned that feelings mostly hurt. Feelings that are good leave you vulnerable. As a child I learned to adopt a sort of hyper vigilance, feeling good only when alone or with friends. My home life was unpredictable and I could never let down my guard or take anyone into my confidence. If I were to tell a secret to anyone in the family it would come back at me when someone else needed to give up chips or wanted to be mean themselves. The nearly daily outrage was when I was summoned to the kitchen table where my father held court over his gin Tom Collins. Stewing over my minor infractions, red faced with his pickled breath, I was informed about how the world works and that I was an ungrateful participant.

"You got a 'B' in math and a 'C' in science. I'm not spending my money on you for these kinds of grades", he yelled.

"But I got an 'A' on everything else", I replied.

Then off came the belt as it always did. A few whacks across the face for the grades and a few more on my ass for talking back. I didn't understand. I tried as hard as I could. I got the best grades out of all the kids in our house at that time. Holding court at the kitchen table often ended in a beating, even if I hadn't done anything wrong. My mother always just stood there, said nothing and watched. Fearful she might endure her own beating I suppose.

I tried my best to please my parents. Like a dog, I continued this quest throughout the beatings and degradation. I was the only one of the older children accepted to private Catholic school. I was the only one of the older children to get straight A's as opposed to D's and F's. My youngest sister was not exposed to the wrath of Tom Collins yet. Nine years younger than me, she stayed out of the fray often taking her meals in her bedroom. My mother tried to protect her but for some reason immunity from the usual forms of abuse was all she could expect. Instead my sister was ignored by my father and resented for being the accident of the family. He tried to put on a good show but continued to get stone cold smashed in her presence as well. Although she was not beaten as the older children, she was shunned in a way that denied her the attention and affection a young girl needs from her father. Later as my father faced his death he softened some towards her but never really offered unconditional love in any fashion especially when it was important.

The holidays of Thanksgiving and Christmas offered no relief to any of the children. Thanksgiving was just an excuse for an all day gin binge. With my alcoholic brother and grandfather home all day and drinking as well there were many fights and bad feelings to go around. The women all stayed in the kitchen and sat around the table not wanting to be part of the fray unfolding in the living room as the hard liquor flowed. As children we were forced to play outside in the cold to avoid getting screamed at for doing nothing on the holiday. If it was raining we were self exiled to our bedrooms until dinner. We later returned there for safety.

Christmas was even worse for me as a child and has often been difficult to manage as an adult. Every year my father would refuse to get a Christmas tree as a putative punishment for some undefined minor infractions that we had committed. I think he took great joy in disappointing us about it. I remember being so upset one year I took some green ribbons from the wrapping supplies and went into my closet. I cried as I cut the ribbons and taped them to the wall to make the shape of a Christmas tree. My tree, one he couldn't take away. My mother saw me and drug me from the closet. When she saw what I had done she asked what I was thinking. I told through the tears. She softened some and told me to play outside saying "If your father sees that he'll give you something to cry about", meaning a severe whipping with the belt.

We got a tree soon after but we were forced to thank my father as if it were a gift only he could bestow on us. Eventually he bought an aluminum tree with a colored light wheel. Then the fight became when to get it from the attic. Most of my life my father painted the house bright pink. Then at Christmas we had a shiny metal tree with changing colors in the window for everyone to see. Sometimes people would ask me where I lived. I would say, "I live up on Hickory Dr."

Invariably they would ask, "Hey, do you live near that pink house with the aluminum Christmas tree?"

I would reply, "Hey man, I live 'in' that pink house with the aluminum Christmas tree."

"What were your parents thinking?" was almost always the astonished reply.

"I have no idea", I would say shaking my head.

It has taken many years to return the joy of Christmas to my life. Still every year is a challenge. The legacy often beats me down. I am still not sure when to get the tree. Some years I have simply gone without one.

# Poor Examples

Some of my siblings set poor examples and little seemed to be expected of them. I had one brother who, like my father, excelled at alcoholism most of his young adult life. I remember many psychotic incidents that took place in and around our house. For example, one bright sunny afternoon my brother got drunk, drove his car up over the curb, burned his tires on the lawn and then rammed his car into the lower concrete foundation of my parent's house. He then stood on the horn with his foot while his upper body stuck out the sun roof and demanded my father come out and answer for all the trouble his drinking had caused. Here was an irony of the legacy where one drunk accuses another drunk for his being drunk himself. No wonder I got confused at a young age.

The best my father could do was come out and tell him to get the car off the lawn then retreat back into the house, have another drink and lower his mood to an even darker place. A day after this incident my brother suddenly appeared at my parent's house sober with his wife in tow and claimed he didn't remember what had happened, total blackout. This, in my parents view, actually exonerated him from wrong doing because all the things that were said and done were driven by the alcohol. He didn't really mean those things, so everything was OK. Denial, denial and more denial. The legacy takes on a life of its own.

Another brother did so poorly in school that a job in a gas station was considered a good career choice for him by my parents. About all he had any aptitude for was wrenching on old broken cars. Not to actually fix them but to make them better in an unquantifiable fashion. I always observed the old broken cars around our house remained pretty much old broken cars even after much work was supposedly done on them. I assume the cars at work faired better as he was using someone else's resources. His uneventful gas station career continued for over 10 years even after several children were born.

He married into a Mormon family where the wife was not expected and even refused to work. They became so poor they received an assisted living allowance from the county (section 8 housing) and food stamps. By this time he had a job at a local car dealership. Perpetually broke, he still had to ask for and received money from my father on a regular basis. Why I don't know. He broke my father's heart when he renounced being Catholic to join the Mormon Church; a necessary step in marrying someone in that faith. Because he was attempting to raise a family he remained the favorite and was given any amount of money he asked for. My father would role over in his grave if he knew some of his grandchildren had spent more than a little time in jail for some very serious offenses. Still in his view of the time, just having children earned the reward, not how they turned out.

My grandmother lived with us for several years and my father would go into my grandmother's room and lift a hundred dollars or more out of her drawer and give it to him. My grandmother kept her Social Security stashed there because she didn't trust banks. She was later put into a home but the money stayed there with her furniture and served as a repository for certain family needs. My needs were excluded of course. Only my mother and father and brother knew it was there. When my father died my mother counted the money and took some for my father's funeral. My grandmother died two weeks later and when my mother went again to get some cash for her funeral most of it, several thousand dollars was gone. She called me in a panic and said she had been robbed. I told her to call the police and I would come right over. When I got there she was alone in the living room.

"When are the police coming", I asked.

"I didn't call them," she muttered. "Nothing else is missing or disturbed. Your brother was the only one who knew the money was there.

I am sure he or his wife took it not thinking your grandmother would die so soon and I would never notice."

She refused to call the police or confront my brother about it. I personally don't know who took the money or how much actually existed but I always assumed my mother was correct by the level of emotion associated with the loss. I did convince her to change the locks on the house and she did. Nothing was ever said about it again until my mother died. According to her, my father would have wanted it that way. He wanted a lot of things when he was alive and some when he was dead. Why she feared his anger fifteen years after he died is mute testament to the power of an abusive alcoholic spouse. Often this performance is channeled into a form of "pretzel logic" where the premise and conclusion make perfect sense to the drunk and the enablers but to no one else.

Some years before he died, my father telephoned me drunk one night. He demanded a "gentleman's agreement" from me. He wanted me to promise I would surrender all claim to my parent's estate upon their death and give it to this particular brother. When I asked why my father simply told me, "he's having children and you're not". I was only 20 years old at the time. I was too young by most standards to start a family. I politely refused and counseled him to put it in his will if that is the way he wanted it. So he did. Fortunately, when he died my mother changed it back to be shared by all the siblings upon her death. In her later years she added a codicil to the will excluding this brother from any inheritance because she felt she had been ripped off by him and his wife. Not just the money from the drawer but other things as well. She told all her friends and some family members she had done this. When she died this codicil was apparently, according to the executor, not included as part of the will. I always wondered what happened to it. Had he been excluded as she wished many of the problems would not have happened. Or had this additional instruction been misunderstood or just been misplaced? Hindsight is 20/20. However, manipulation comes from all angles as a rule of the legacy, so I don't know what to believe or if I should render blame.

# Life is Unpredictable

Examples of unpredictable abuse abound in the stories told by an alcoholic's children. Although I remember most of them with vivid detail, some everyday incidents I have blocked out because of the pain. Most will not be mentioned here as they are numerous and repetitious. The following is a typical example of what I remember.

In 1969 as a freshman in Catholic high school much was expected of me. My grades, clothing, attitude were all scrutinized by my parents and by school officials. On a rare occasion one could commune with the Christian Brothers on an informal almost equal level. Field trips were one of these occasions. There was a field trip available after school to go to San Francisco to see a play. About an hours drive away, it gave students a chance to see our teachers in another light. How they drove a car for example was telling of their secret inner personality, or so we thought. On this afternoon/evening excursion we went to see a play entitled *Hadrian the Seventh*. It was a remarkable experience for me as I had never been to the city to see a play. I was stunned by the performances, the costumes and the exquisite air of walking through the city at night, its streets glistening and wet. It was like a walk through a movie with all the sounds and smells of the city overwhelming me. It was a time when I was feeling good and I felt anything might be possible.

Back at home trouble was waiting for me. My parents had decided to buy me a winter coat instead of handing one down which was the norm. The week before, my mother and I had gone to Wards and picked one out but could not buy it until my father approved. While I was at the play, my mother had gone back to the store to buy it but as usual bought one extra large thinking, as always, I would somehow grow into it. Around 9:00 P.M. Brother John dropped me off at home. My father was smashed and began to yell at me for coming home late from school. My mother tried to change the subject by getting me to try on the new coat. It was obviously far too big. When I said so, my father screamed at me like I had just killed Jesus myself.

"It's your fault the coat is too big. If you hadn't been out fucking around all night you could have been there and got the right coat", he shrieked. "You are the most ungrateful piece of shit in this house. I'm not wasting good money on you. You can just wear that coat or go without."

His face was red and the stench of all day hard liquor drinking and cigarettes permeated the room. I was forbidden to go on field trips again and put on restriction. Reasonable people just exchange coats that are too big. Alcoholics need to punish someone for such things. It was many years later I found out that merchandise is returned and exchanged everyday without any penalty to the buyer. Even as a child I felt it was all so unfair and as an adult I began to rage at the blame laid on me for nothing. In the end I was forced to wear the coat. If I wore four sweaters underneath it almost fit me.

Growing up in this house was so unpredictable. My father's drinking often set him off to rage about unimportant and irrelevant issues. Often when I was summoned to the Court of Tom Collins at the kitchen table my mother would follow. She would stand behind me and parrot all my answers to his questions to make sure they were heard and acceptable.

One year as a late birthday present I received a cassette tape recorder I had wanted. I had asked for it for 2 years before but when money is tight you can't always get what you want. I eagerly opened the package and put the batteries in. It was a very nice recorder. I started to experiment with it when I was summoned to the kitchen table to suffer through an interrogation of how I liked my birthday present. I had to appear and present the gift opened in front of him as he wasn't really sure what I had just received. I deliberately hit the record button and recorded to whole conversation.

"Is that what you wanted", my father asked?

"It's more than I wanted", I said.

"What", my father snapped?

"It's more than he wanted", my mother repeated.

"Can you use it for anything", he asked?

"I can use it for lots of things", I said excitedly.

"What", he snapped again?

"He can use it for lots of things", my mother repeated again.

It was sickening. This form of communication was common in our house as my father asked the questions but wasn't really interested in our answers. He just wanted to show his control over us. My mother did the follow up and often we were dismissed and she finished the conversation for us. I recently found a box of old tapes that contained this conversation. I wasn't sure if I wanted to keep it but after realizing it was the only recording I have of their voices I put it back in its place and left it to discover another day.

# *Impact of Religion*

I was raised in a Catholic house. My father was the product of a Catholic orphanage school where he was put during the depression by his own alcoholic parents. I began to see the hypocrisy of dogma and creed very early in life, but my fear of hell kept me from verbalizing this thought to anyone. Remember, I could trust no one. Catechism, first communion and confession were all part of my upbringing. My parents wanted me to be a priest. I finally achieved part of their goals by getting accepted to a private Catholic high school. Pressure was constantly exerted to consider the seminary. I liked girls far too much to give it all up before I had my first date. My father had a medieval sense of worship. The first son stayed with the land, the second went to the King and the third to the church. I was the third. But the first and second didn't fall into the paradigm, why should I?

About the time I was 13 years old, I was told at Catechism we were to be confirmed Catholic. It was not automatic however, we had to make a choice. We were told at our age young men can make their own decisions about their religious convictions. We were to make our own choice to be confirmed or not. I chose not to. That's when I learned choosing not to be confirmed was not a choice I was being given. I thought it was. After all they made it very clear.

At the first notice I gave against confirmation, I was severely reprimanded by the teacher at the time, bitch Sister Frances. She took me out of class and into the boys' bathroom where a boy was at the urinal relieving himself. She started to slap the side of my head over and over. So hard in fact she finally knocked me down. The boy at the urinal tripped over me as he tried to run out, zipper down and a big wet spot on his pants from being unable to stop peeing as he stashed the goods.

"How stupid are you?" she screamed. "You are going to Hell for even thinking those thoughts, do you know that? God has given you a great gift and you turn away to evil. You will be punished forever."

And then she began to hit me with the yardstick she brought until it broke in two. I was then drug by the ear to the rectory to see the vicious Monsignor Hennessy, a distance of about one city block. I think my ear never regained its shape. To make matters worse Monsignor Hennessy was the most pompous, arrogant son of a bitch that ever wore a purple cumber bun. When he heard I was considering not becoming confirmed, he grabbed me by the shoulder and pinched my flesh so hard I cried. The bruising from this lasted for weeks. He never asked why I was considering this. He walked me to the open door of the rectory and threw me through it onto the landing at the top of the stairs.

"Don't ever come to this place of God without proper respect and penance. Go to confession now and tell your confessor about your evil thoughts." He slammed the door behind me. Bitch Sister Frances was waiting for me on the sidewalk. As I approached her she attempted to assault me again by grabbing me by the hair. When I fought her off she became enraged and followed me to the church. Before I went into the confessional, she knocked on the door and had a short conference with the priest inside. My confession was predictably short.

I told the priest, "I was given a choice and the people who gave me the choice say I made the wrong one and now want to take that choice away. I don't understand why I should be beaten for my choice. It's as if I had been lied to."

In a low voice the priest responded, "Say six Rosaries and think about two things, your life in Hell forever and your so called choice you think you have made. You will do as you are told. You are clearly not mature enough to make this choice on your own."

The school made a call home and I got another beating from my father when I got there, a severe whipping with the belt, his favorite thing. This dispute about confirmation went on for several weeks until finally there was a meeting between my father, the lesser Priest and the bitch Sister Frances. I was told I would have one chance to ask any question I wanted about the religion, clear up all my doubts and then I was to make my decision again, hopefully to be confirmed.

I asked, "If religion is about good and Jesus taught about love, why must I be beaten until I believe in good and love? It seems that hitting me will not bring me closer to the church that forces me to say what they want me to say and not say what I believe."

The lesser Priest replied, "What you believe is wrong and you are being punished because your thoughts are evil. You are an ungrateful son of our Lord God and Jesus. You will suffer in Hell for your actions. Now you are being given a chance to clear up your questions and join the great family of God, so ask your questions. There will not be another chance."

So I asked, "How did Jesus make seven fish into a thousand?"

The lesser Priest was annoyed but said, "It was a miracle".

I was silent for a long time and then the bitch Sister asked, "don't you believe in miracles?"

I very softly replied, "It's hard to believe in miracles when someone is pulling your hair out by its roots".

The lesser Priest stood up and said, "Unless you have more faith than that, you will suffer in Hell forever. If you die before you have faith, no one can save you, you are doomed".

He left the room as did the bitch Sister. My father stood up and said let's go. On the way home he informed me I would be confirmed the following Saturday. I told him I wouldn't, it was my choice. He back handed me across the mouth and said, "On Saturday morning you put on a white shirt and go to the Church, get in line and be confirmed and that's that. You don't need to do anything or say anything, just do it." My nose and mouth bleeding I went to my room crying. I vowed to return the favor by not being confirmed and perhaps punish his sense of righteous religious arrogance at all costs. I couldn't believe he was in support of these parochial idiots instead of me. On other occasions he would refer to them as "psalm singing hypocrites" in spite of his putative adherence to sacramental devotion.

On Saturday morning I got up early, left the house on my bike at 6 A.M. before anyone was awake. I did not return home until 11 P.M. I didn't put on the white shirt and I didn't get confirmed. Faith had nothing to do with it. I had reached an age where I refused to be beaten into submission for any reason. My father didn't speak to me for weeks. The subject of confirmation never came up again. Amazingly, I went on to Catholic high school. It seemed that after all the violent opposition to my decision; confirmation was not a prerequisite for admission.

In hindsight I believe my outspoken nature and penchant for trouble also saved me from any sexual abuse by the clergy. It seems pedophile priests prefer quiet more docile boys. I actually know some boys who suffered this form of sexual abuse, including rape. At the time I was unaware of this type of abuse and that at least two of my friends were suffering as a result of it. Many years later a very close friend of mine in middle school revealed to me at our 25th high school reunion he had sex (man/boy) with our language teacher on a regular basis. "He was the first one I had sex with", he said to me. In all I am aware of four teachers, lay and clergy mixed who were convicted of sex with or molestation of minors in their classes. I have heard rumors of others but, I have no evidence to prove it. At one time or another I had to take at least one class with all of these teachers. I even went to the same mass every Sunday at the Oakland Cathedral as the language teacher in question. I always noticed the pain on his face when he prayed. Now I know it was the look of guilt. Although this type of sexual abuse didn't happen to me, I think I would prefer to be beaten as I was rather than be forced to have sex with my teachers. It's shocking to me knowing my friends were abused in this way.

Being in Catholic high school in the late 1960's was a trial in itself. However, I began to feel a better connection with my religion for the first time in the high school environment. The Vietnam War was a raging, festering sore on the skin of America. Anti-war sentiment was encouraged at school and the weekly folk mass became a connecting point to my peers. Even though I found that the church was not interested in helping me with my troubles at home, I found some peace. After all, in a predominately Irish Catholic community, a drink was acceptable. Many drinks a luxury. But at this new school there was a focus on the individual as the hope for the future. We were taught not to judge others harshly but to make the world better in our own image; the clean image of the young studious Christian gentleman. It was a transparent fallacy but it empowered me to see beyond the seemingly insurmountable problems at home and to seek the divine within. For me the divine is a very small place inside where it is quiet. However, in the alcoholic legacy every blue sky has a dark cloud hiding somewhere.

I lasted in Catholic school for about two years. In the summer of 1971 I woke up and realized I had been working far too hard at something that may be meaningless. I had struggled through my sophomore year after missing two months of school from contracting mononucleosis. For the most part I was holding to my usual good grades but was suffering in biology. The teacher called my mother and told her I would have to make up the class in summer school if I received a failing grade as it was a required course. I finished the year and my final exam in biology without knowing what the final grade would be. My mother informed me a few days later that the biology teacher had called and I failed the course. So off I went to summer school to make up the required class. I finished summer school with a 'B' in biology. Then some days after it was all over I accidentally found my report card from Catholic school lying under the blotter on the desk in the dining room. I was told by my parents that it hadn't arrived. Yet there it was, good grades for the entire term including a 'B' in the original biology class I had supposedly failed. My parents had lied to me. When I confronted my mother about the deception she just smiled and said, "It never hurts to do better if you can". I missed out on half my summer because my parents deliberately lied to me. It was the last time I ever fully trusted my mother again.

I made the announcement I would quit Catholic school and return to public school where I belonged. I basically refused to produce the kudos my parents reaped at my expense. I was also exhausted from the continual references to a seminary I had no intention of attending. By the time I was half way through high school it was a known fact there was quite a bit of homosexual activity going on at the remote location. The seminary was someone else's trip I couldn't buy into. It became a difficult time in our house. Instead of verbal abuse and the signature whipping I got a new form of abuse; the silent treatment. My father did not speak to me for weeks. My mother was also angry with me because when my father was not happy, no one was happy. They never understood how I felt about being lied to. In their opinion I was not allowed the luxury of demanding accountability from anyone especially them. With this decision to leave Catholic school I became the one who disappointed everyone in everyway. Without my parents help I registered myself and then I returned to public school and a long needed breath of air.

# Public School

Nothing can match the comfort the invisibility of public high school brought to me. You can be anything you want in public school. The high expectations of private school can narrow the vision of even the greatest genius and therefore, creativity can languish. This can also happen in public school when the expectations of well intentioned people collide with the playful and innocent nature of a child. I was tested early in life and branded a "gifted child" by a psychologist because of my higher than average I.Q.. A term my parents misunderstood to mean "one who should do extra homework", something I fought for many years. My parents didn't know the difference between capacity and creativity.

For an early example of this I'll take you back to 1963. When I was in the third grade I was being considered for a grade skip to fourth. There was a trial period of a week. I was put ahead into the fourth grade to see if I could produce at that level. Everything went well until one day at recess. I ran to play with my third grade friends who were involved in a vigorous game of dodge ball. I was stopped by the fourth grade teacher and reprimanded.

"You must play on this field. Those aren't your friends anymore", she said. "Learn to make new friends in your new class." She added tersely, "If you must talk to them, do it after school. You don't want people to think you are not ready to skip grades."

So I tried to play with the older kids who called me names like baby boy and third grader. I longed for all the good fun I had at the creek with my third grade friend Jimmy. We played army and killed imaginary Nazis, caught frogs and learned about new things at our own speed. Now the older kids seemed like the Nazis. At the end of the week the teachers and the principal had a meeting with my mother and me. With big smiles on their faces I was asked how I liked moving up a grade.

I told them, "the home work wasn't hard but I don't understand why I can't play with my friends anymore. It seems to me fourth grade is like third grade without your friends." The principal told me, "you can play with those kids anytime you want as long as it is after school. Skipping a grade is an honor not all children are considered for and you should be grateful."

Well it seemed to me I had been told already on numerous occasions how ungrateful I was for all the things I had. Now the principal was telling me the same thing. I didn't realize at the time I had buttons that could be pushed. The rest of the meeting I said nothing even when asked. This was a grown up game set up by my parents and I wasn't prepared to play it. I was interrogated by the fourth grade teacher and told to respond to the questions being asked. I remember how I started to cry. My mother asked me what was wrong and I couldn't respond to her either. My third grade teacher, a visionary angel named Mrs. Redding took me outside and asked me quietly if all this was too much for me. I shook my head yes through the tears and she said, "Ok, you're with me for the rest of the year, if you want to be. You can stay in my class where you can be with the people you know. Creative kids like you need more than extra home work."

So with all the other people involved concluding I wasn't ready for the fourth grade I returned to the third. I was grateful but, according to them, for the wrong reason. I was told and made to feel as if I had failed everyone, my parents and teachers. Even at that early age I had a sense of the disappointment I generated by the unnecessary expectations of others. I remember wanting to expand my life, not excel in it. I did continue to excel in school, although it was never again recognized by my parents. I was sometimes reminded "you had your chance to skip a grade but you turned it down". It was many years later I realized

I should never have accepted my educational direction from my father; a man who never formally graduated from high school.

To move on with the story let's go back to 1971 again. After returning to public high school, I quietly went to class with the masses of people. The new school had over 2000 students whereas the school I came from had only 400. My junior year was uneventful and I got good grades. I auditioned for and obtained leading roles in both term plays my senior year. Prior to returning to public school I had been withdrawn and introverted. This changed as I pushed myself out of obscurity and onto the stage. This was a great risk for someone in my position. The second term play, *The Miser*, by Moliere was a great success. I played Harpagon the miser. After the last night of the play I was out in the crowd. People were all around me laughing and patting me on the back and telling me what a great job I had done. Then I saw something coming at me from the side. It looked like a tall red faced ogre with my mother in tow. It was my father. From twelve feet away I could see that red face, hear his heavy breathing and smell the stench of a drunk on an all day binge.

"Now I know how you waste your time," he boomed for the entire crowd to hear. The room fell silent as he walked away, my mother following, fighting back the tears. She said nothing to me.

"Who was that," someone asked?

"My father," I said disgustingly.

"Why did he say that," someone else asked?

I said nothing. There was nothing to say.

Although still struggling with personal problems, when I graduated I received the year's Best Actor award for that play and a 4.0 straight A average for the term. When I did it only for me it was easy. When I tried to do it all for others, I never reached their expectations. The theater helped me gain a better sense of myself for many years to come in spite of the resounding objections from my father. It was very hard for me as a teenager to suffer under such continual criticism just before I made my way into the world on my own. I always hated him for that as well as other things.

# Personal Despair and Victimization

**B**y this time I had my drivers license and even though I managed well in some areas I was not in the clear emotionally. During this period I developed a sense of identification with the situation at home and a great despair of self emerged. When the role models in my life did not behave in acceptable ways, it was hard to see a life any other way. In those days I thought if your parents act funky, it must be acceptable. After high school I moved out of the house and started smoking pot on a regular basis to ease the pain. It seemed to work and continued for many years.

Interestingly enough, many of my friends had no idea that there was a drinking problem in our house. Sometimes I would really question if there was, only to realize that it was a secret that we kept. As a child, there is a danger of embarrassing yourself if you embarrass your parents. I began to question the perceptual reality of my putative life. The process of doing this caused me incredible despair for many years. Bringing family problems into the light was not acceptable until recent years. However, after most of my family died and the others abandoned me there was little danger in it. In fact in some circles such revelations are now quite fashionable.

After many years of youthful despair I began to believe life was filled with pervasive inconsistent unpredictability. And subsequently that's why my father was a drinker. Nearly three decades later that I found evidence to show his problems were much deeper than I thought. They had other roots extending back to his early childhood. More importantly life, as well as the world around me, would not turn out to be as I was taught.

The process of victimization had started long before this time and continued for many years to come. Victimization is an inevitable creation of being abused in the alcoholic legacy. As a battered and abused child I developed a sense of being put down so much that I eventually developed into a victim. Although I actually was a victim, I came to see myself as a victim of every situation where I did not come out ahead. This occurred in school, jobs, and personal relationships. If something went wrong with the relationship, I blamed others for their faults and not myself. Truthfully, victims need others to be at fault because as children they were made into victims and no other process of conflict resolution is readily available. The victim identity never leaves until a formerly battered individual sees the process and makes an attempt to overcome this personal deficit. Many alcoholics also buy into the victimization model. This occurs generally when they as children were made to feel less than they were or blamed for things they did not control. Victimization is a common holdover from the alcoholic upbringing and transposes itself into the lives of those who were abused. It is one thing shared by the abuser and the abused. They will both buy into the victim identity at some time during their lives and relationships.

It occurred to me this book is the product of victimization. With all the stories of being abused and references to my failures being caused by others, blame squarely resting on the drinking parent and others. It is true I buy into this and this book may present itself in that fashion. My decision to publish was dampened by the thought of it. I didn't want to be a victim anymore and yet I was spilling my guts about how it all came down. And it really wasn't my fault, none of it. Sounds like a victim to me. Yet, all the stories are true. They really happened. I am left with a puzzle to reassemble. At the risk of sounding like a victim and conscious of this fact I continued to write in an attempt to finally document and purge the identity from deep within me. It has been a long and cumbersome project.

# The World Around Me

When I was young I was often puzzled by the world around me. The outside world seemed ordered and peaceful and beckoned me to dream and hope for many things. I played with my friend Jimmy and others, rode bikes and passionately wondered about the outer world beyond my comprehension. I was allowed a birthday party every few years and went to many parties for my friends. I wrote with chalk on the sidewalk and climbed a lot of trees. I really enjoyed riding the shiny blue ten speed I bought with the money from my paper route. I watched with enthusiasm as the older kids in the neighborhood approached their teenage years and began to form many ideas about how I wanted my life to look at that age. What clothes I might wear and the car I might drive. Even what kind of girl I might like to date, not that I was in any hurry for that.

The inner world, my home life, was far removed from my everyday dreams. It seemed to be in a constant state of conflict with itself. Here was an undercurrent of chaos and perpetual turmoil of which I was often blamed as the cause. My father fostered an air of contempt for everyone and everything except Edmund G. (Pat) Brown the former governor of California. Creativity and my particular genius of vision had no place in this home world. I began to keep my hopes and dreams to myself. This was the beginning of my sick period of introversion. I was afraid of having my feelings hurt or being ridiculed for thinking outside the box. These were instinctual acts as I was too young to intellectually understand the machinations of alcoholism and child abuse.

I remember an incident in the garage where my father and one of my brothers were arguing about something. My mother, another brother and I went out to see what was going on. We arrived in time to see my brother take a half ass swing at my father to try to hit him. My father grabbed him and while holding him against the shelving screamed at my mother, "get in the house and take the boys with you."

Not two minutes later my brother came in the back door crying, his nose and mouth bleeding. My father followed him in. Pushing us out of the way he trailed my brother to his bedroom, slammed the door and began shouting at him for the longest time. It was beyond my comprehension as an eight year old but I now know and understand my father had just beaten the shit out of one of my brothers. Some months later I asked my mother why my father hated my older brother. Also why did he say he was stupid for joining the army?

My mother told me, "Never talk about this with your father. Some things should never leave this house either. These are things you don't understand. Promise me you will never tell anyone what goes on in this house. What goes on in someone's house is nobody's business but their own. Don't forget it". Therein lies the problem, I haven't forgotten it.

Soon after that my brother went off to Fort Ord. I remember seeing him for the last time before he left. I cried as I saw him there in his new green uniform. I don't know why I cried but I think I was afraid for him and sad for myself. My brother seemed happy with the decision but later I found out he wanted to go to Vietnam to prove something to my father. Either he would be a man and fight in a war or he would be killed and get even with the old man by causing him pain. Neither thing happened as my brother caught a debilitating form of pneumonia and was released on a medical discharge and never saw combat duty. Joining the National Guard after that didn't exactly impress my father either.

It was on one of his National Guard weekends away that the most interesting incident between my father and brother happened. My mother called me to say I needed to help my father with something and to come home right away. I was about 18 years old at the time. My brother had gone away to his duty weekend but got severely drunk and belligerent with his commanding officer. Then he apparently left the base in his car. He was returned to the base by the Military Police as they had some jurisdiction over him because he was on duty. To make a long story short, I was to drive my father to the base because he had been drinking too much that day and then drive my brother's car to my house so he didn't have access to it. My father was supposed to sober on the 2 hour drive to this particular location. We hardly spoke the whole trip.

When we arrived at the army base, my brother was standing in the parking lot handcuffed to a military police car with an armed MP watching over him. He was stinking drunk, crying and blurting out blame on my father for his current predicament. My father was suddenly sober. The embarrassment alone nearly killed him. I got my brother's car and took off some time ahead of them and tried to forget about what had just happened. It was after all a very nice day and the little sports car was fun to drive. I hated that I had to be involved in this incident. "What's it going to be next?" I thought as I slowly meandered home. Predictably the next day my brother claimed 'black out' again and was exonerated from wrong doing by my parents. Then I was accused of racing his car home and damaging it somehow. You just can't do anything right as a child in an alcoholic house, even when you try to help someone.

My brother was married to his high school sweetheart and for years struggled greatly with his own alcoholism battle that ended only after my father had died. I would say I talk to him occasionally but the truth is we haven't talked in years. One of the last times we spoke on the phone was Christmas Eve several years ago. He was in a hurry and couldn't talk. He said he was late to a party at another brother's house. A party I wasn't invited to. Because I haven't seen him, his Christmas presents for the last few years are on the table behind me as I write this. Eventually I will mail them as I have done in the past. Sometimes I feel his passage in life has been worse than mine. But in our last conversation he told me, "It is easier to tell myself I'll deal with it later and then not deal with it at all". While he buries his head in the sand he must not realize time is quickly passing us by.

This attitude is typical in the alcoholic legacy. Editing recollections is often another form of denial with a piece of a lie attached to it in the way you get dog shit attached to you shoe. Editing "the stories as it were" was practiced regularly in our house. My parents didn't exactly keep us insulated or protected from the outside world but often filtered the information and consequences of events in an opaque form of denial to meet their own perception of reality. When a man I had never heard of, Dr. Martin Luther King Jr., was killed, I asked my father who he was.

He replied, "Oh, some trouble maker."

My father was far from being a racist and in fact often fought where he worked to defend and promote blacks. But all color aside, he didn't understand the nature of the selfless act nor people who sacrificed their lives for one. He was manic depressive and bipolar and his perception of the outside world meant it was made up of people who were not real, only reported to be real. Like Don Quixote fighting the windmill, my parents fought with their perception of truth and its inherent reality as if it were some evil thing never to be disturbed. They were dealing with too much evil as it was, and somewhere in the dark part of themselves they knew it. It was deeply rooted in the secrets they kept. Refusing to be openly accountable is the darkest part of human treachery; the loss of truth and the ability to experience it.

My parents would say Don Quixote was crazy. To me amid the chaos, he would become a hero. He was all Quixote, all the time; a constant in search of a solution regardless of consequence. Just and full of passion he lived his perception of reality in no uncertain terms. In our house there was no search for solutions, only the fallout from the failure to accept consequence and embrace accountability. The only constant in my life growing up was alcoholism and the attempt to hide it at any cost. Such is the legacy I inherited.

In an alcoholic household there is no predictability, no honesty, and no claim to humility upon defeat. No equation to a final solution. Even the crazy man Don Quixote had that. If our perceived reality is all we have, mine became poisoned at a very early age. Insanity was the only thing to be shared with my mythical hero.

It has taken decades to face up to the fact I grew up to be much like my father. Abusive and hateful colored with great contempt for those who had ever done anything to hurt me. I have often hated myself for who I have become almost as much as I have hated my father. The struggle in the process of recovery is to learn forgiveness for myself and for others. However, it is like saying, "other than that Mr. Lincoln how was the play?" It is a sad state of affairs when a wicked word play describes how I feel. But there it is.

I originally didn't see this as a book with a happy ending but I want it to be. This is not a book about heroes but rather a book about me as a troubled person and the solutions I seek. Maybe it is a book about a hero. The one I hope to become someday, the hero who saved his own life.

# PART II

# Letters from My Father

M y parents are both dead now. As a result of my mother's death in 1998 I came into possession of something I had never expected to receive; vindication. One of the very few things I received from my parents' estate was a box of letters from my father to my mother. There were about 160 of them written while he was in the army from February 1943 to January 1945. They record my father's obsessive thoughts and abusive behavior in a constant cold stream of words I couldn't believe I was reading. My mother had some design that I should get these letters as the box containing them was sealed with "Karl, do not open before I am gone, Mom" written on the bottom. After reading a few of the letters I was so disturbed I put the box in a large trunk and put it into storage.

This bequest and its meaning haunted me and for about a year and the letters remained unread. I had no desire to discover any soft romantic side of my father and I feared further "from the grave" manipulation from my mother the enabler. After reading the letters I learned there was no soft romantic side to my father and as far as "from the grave" manipulation goes, I still do not know what to think. I had been so angry for so long at the thought that I could have, as a child, disappointed my father so much. That he should expect so much, despise me and criticize all that I would do. My mother did her best to support us, maybe even protect us but the enabler always defers to the drinker. I wanted nothing to do with either of them. I wanted his written ramblings to mean nothing to me.

One day I realized at the core of anger is always some fact whether real or imagined. I didn't believe I had imagined all the abuse, certainly not the beatings but, maybe I had imagined his intention. Maybe there was none, just abusive behavior. All grist for the mill now, he escaped by dying in 1983 at a relatively young 62 years old. I also believe he welcomed death as a release from his own confusion about life.

It always seemed so unfair that even as I excelled in school, the abuse continued for the smallest of infractions and often for no reason at all. I learned to hate at a time I should have learned to play baseball and look to the future. Instead I was often expected to predict when I was to speak, how to act at all times, come home from school and most of all stay out of the way. I was envied and hated by a brother who was my father's favorite. My attempts to stay out of trouble were often sabotaged by my siblings to protect themselves from beatings. Everybody in my house lied. It was a survival game. The lies continued even during the disposition of my mother's belongings and would continue today had I not split from those who continue in this behavior.

Then these letters appeared. What should I think about these letters? I looked over the box one day and I realized it had been opened since my mother showed it to me. I remembered it had been taped shut but was only held together by a couple of rubber bands when delivered to me. One of my brothers and his wife claimed they opened it to look for the life insurance that didn't exist. In the same manner, with the same excuse they opened an envelope that said "Karl's first haircut 1956". When held to the light it revealed only hair. But it was torn in half anyway and I can't now be sure if it really is my hair or some joke they wish to play on me. After all these are the people that destroyed most of my pictures as a child, took the frames and sought to secretly destroy anything I might enjoy as an adult.

So with great trepidation I began to read the letters. Again, I was shocked at the content. I realized right off that this man was a monster long before, some twelve years before, I was born. But why was he this way? My own hatred turned to frustration and more anger. In my world this type of crisis turns my thoughts to danger, constant danger. I was exhausted from it. It consumed my life and destroyed my own relationships. I once heard that the Chinese write the word crisis with two characters. One stands for danger and the other for opportunity. In my life I have seen and experienced much crisis. Until recently I perceived only danger in the world. Today, finally, I seek the opportunity crisis brings.

Through a great many years of mental and emotional struggle, coupled of course by a few years of substance abuse, I sought help from many professionals who at best only wanted to tackle a piece of the problem. I was finally able to recognize the destructive thoughts and anger I had coveted as one of my only possessions. I was finally able to start rebuilding from the beginning. The letters became a way to understand how abuse in a family can start. I am not talking now about my immediate family but rather, my father's.

As it turns out his childhood was much like mine only with more despair, alcoholism and rejection from his parents. At one point He writes that he is so ashamed of how his parents live that he told everyone he knew at boot camp his parents lived on a farm far away. When he got leave he would steal away to see the parents and not tell anyone where he had gone. Often the visit would end when they asked him for money. His stated intention for the visit sometimes was to borrow money from them. He often recorded who owed who and how much to the penny. The truth of his childhood has been told in pieces for years. Now there was some cohesion.

During the depression, my father was sent to live at a Catholic orphanage because his parents couldn't feed two children. His older brother was the favorite and so my father was sent away. The older brother died of a brain tumor when he was 12 years old. But my father was apparently never retrieved from the facility. When he was in his late teens, his father ran off from Denver to California with another woman. My father left the school, loaded his mother on a bus, and came to California to find his father. In Oakland they found him and somehow tried to resume some sort of family life. My grandfather and grandmother were alcoholics and my father had to work to support them as they couldn't or wouldn't get jobs. This went on for many years.

Sometime at the end of 1942 while working in the shipyards in Richmond my father met my mother. Around the same time the strain of supporting his parents became too much for him. To escape, my father joined the army just as my brother did. Shortly before he shipped off to boot camp he became engaged to my mother while drunk one night. He writes of this night and admonishes my mother for accepting a proposal from someone who was "tight", a common term for having too much to drink. The pontificating expressed in these documents is enormous and between the lines the tragedy and sadness of his existence show through.

The issues the man confronted me with during my upbringing have their roots in his own childhood and are expressed in no uncertain terms in these letters. Volumes could be written about every letter but I feel reticent to do so because of the diverse and sometimes non sequator nature of the subject matter. Indeed there is enough material to write another book (which I may do someday). However, since I find it important to explore the origins of hateful feelings I will share some of the more important points and how they relate to me. Where they came from and how they transposed themselves into my life when I would have otherwise grown into a more forgiving person from the outset. An outline of the key issues expressed in these letters and the relevance to the legacy are listed below.

# 1. MONEY, WHAT'S MINE AND WHAT'S MINE

Everyone has a need, even a struggle to own something in life. My father worked at several jobs to support his drunken parents and never really accumulated anything of his own save his contempt of others and regret. Money trouble plagued him in the letters with comments about how he owed to other soldiers, lost in gambling, the army didn't come through with the correct pay and on and on. He even supposedly borrowed money from his own parents which I know is not true. They had no money. He used the lack of money as an excuse not to visit my mother on leave, not to send her the engagement ring he promised, and how he couldn't get pictures developed. Money and the lack of it was a convenient excuse. He often wrote about how he would save a certain amount of money to buy a house for them. But this house had to be the one he thought was perfect as he wrote women have no clue of such things. He often insulted her in his letters because she didn't send him more money when he needed it. Telling her "women can't manage money"; he chastised her for not meeting his financial expectations. This criticism went on all through their marriage and my childhood. Why she put up with it I don't know.

After the war he worked at a few different jobs including one with the sheriff's department. America and all his family history were eventually too much for him and he moved my mother and oldest brother to Australia to live. A new dream for him and a new start in a country he had spent time in during the war. The local Australian papers wrote of the American sheriff who hung up his guns to come to Australia to be an accountant. Less than a year later they were back in the United States. My mother said it was because she and my brother were sick all the time from the environment. My father blamed my mother for not being able to be away from her mother. The real reason they came back was unknown. The fact is he always resented my mother for being close to and liking her family. He hated to come back and have to deal with his.

From then on he was in a position of supporting our family never again really having anything of his own. According to him not even his dignity. Hence, we were confronted with his issues around "my money". In reality the issues about every other problem in his life were put onto the money issue as a convenient excuse not to deal with the other problems. Much the way I have in life. The money excuse puzzle was one that took me years to unravel and see for what it was.

## 2. BROKEN PROMISES

He offered and rescinded both marriage proposals and declarations of love to my mother a dozen times in the letters. One day he professed love and later said he could never love a woman like my mother. One day he would write how she was the only thing he could ever think of for the future, then he would write it would be better to not make any plans for the future as his commander advised. They had apparently seen an army film about how to deal with the girl at home. He promised to send her an engagement ring on several occasions. He would say he was not sending it because my mother didn't write enough letters or didn't mail them until two days after they were dated at the top. He claimed he was short of money. After about two years he actually ran out of excuses and started in on telling her he didn't love her in a way that he could marry her. Pitiful excuses for broken promises.

He offered the promise of a stable home through the activities of the church but acted otherwise and unaccountably so. I parlayed broken promises into a failure to commit in relationships. Similar to broken promises, my actions held the hope of future dreams over the heads of others only to run away at a later time for some imagined excuse. I was never sure why I did this until I read the letters and then realized I had learned the fight or flight routine from my father. It is part of the alcoholic legacy. I learned it doesn't take a strong man to run away from a good woman.

## 3. ALCOHOLISM DENIED

He talked and wrote about alcohol but never addressed his problem with it. He often expressed his triumph in gambling as well as his bad luck. Although gambling was something he discussed in his letters it was presented as a right of passage for a soldier to do so. His love affair with gambling took on a different color when we were children. He and my mother, and sometimes he alone, would do an all night trip to

Reno and then drive home broke. He never won as much as he lost and we were truly sheltered from the statistical details. Later I discovered gamblers are given free drinks when they pour money into slot machines. How convenient for a gambling alcoholic.

He never sought recovery from severe alcoholism nor apologized for his failures in self control. I was forced to deny my feeling around alcoholism for many years as a child. Later I denied it happened in our house at all. Still later I denied my own addictive nature to specific behaviors as well as substances. Classic behavior instilled by the legacy. I often think about what he would have become had he attempted some form of recovery. Unfortunately, he never really admitted to anyone he had a problem, the first step in resolving this type of problem.

## 4. BIPOLAR, OBSESSIVE COMPULSIVE BEHAVIOR

One letter is upbeat and the next day depressed, the same day another letter upbeat. He often wrote more than one letter a day about the critical of failure of others to be as upbeat and obsessive as he was about writing letters. He would write that a former coworker had not returned a letter he had written some weeks before and then ordered my mother to look this person up and find out why they have not written back. He would ask my mother to write letters to others for him including a former girlfriend. Then he would ask others including said former girlfriend to write to my mother. It was very strange to read these particular ramblings and requests as some of the people mentioned were not really good friends of my father or mother. They were just people for my father to latch onto in a needy moment. And although I suppose this is to be expected from a war time G.I. Joe, it was inappropriate behavior by my father's later standards. However, I can personally relate to the roller coaster ride of emotions while living with this man and plead guilty to having such needy feelings starting as a teenager and ending sometime in my 30's. I had the need to spend time with anyone who would listen and the need to impress upon them my particular agenda; the need to act out my sickness.

# 5. THREATS OF INFIDELITY AS A MANIPULATION OF MY MOTHER

In the letters he always talked about a woman name Maryanne from Denver who was his friend. He used his friendship with Maryanne to threaten my mother into agreement on certain issues such as how many children to have by saying "Maryanne says this" or "Maryanne says that". Or "maybe I might find another blond who wants what I do". He ordered my mother to write to her and asked Maryanne to write back with all the details of her upcoming wedding to a guy called Coog. Included were descriptions of what dress to where and all that. He even sent Maryanne's picture to my mother and then ordered her to send it back to him in the South Pacific. I nearly threw up when I read this. On one trip to Colorado as a child I met Maryanne's mother and met her brother Bud in California at another time. Maryanne never surfaced to us in anyway on our trips back to Denver where my father was born and raised or at anytime in California where we lived. I wondered for years who she was and later figured it out. My father had on occasion made some trips to Denver alone when we were children. On some of our trips to Denver he took time to himself and disappeared alone for several hours. Some secrets reveal themselves. My father was a cad to use her in this way.

# 6. DOUBLE STANDARD OF THE CHURCH DENIED

Jesus preached love and acceptance but my father's form of love was a bargaining tool to stave off abuse and rejection. In his letters he would often pontificate to my mother and tell her if she was a Catholic she would know how to handle problems at home. As Norwegian immigrants my grandparents were sectarian Lutherans. My grandparents didn't like my father because he was a Catholic and because they recognized his abusive nature. My father often had rude things to say about them. Included in this were their lack of money and my grandfather's alleged lack of ambition to do anything in life. Then he would write how my mother should pray for the intersession or St. Anne (the Virgin Mary's mother) and others.

"So what," I thought as I read this. These musings were like an alter boy parroting his lessons to the local priest to be the one who rings the cool bells at mass. Reading the sickening repetition of Catholic school boy rhetoric caused me to wonder how his devotion was obtained; through faith or physical abuse. My father never spoke of the abuse of the clergy and I often wondered if he wasn't molested himself at the hands of pedophiles. It would figure nicely as a supplemental rage coupled with that of having alcoholic parents. These of course are subjects his generation never spoke of openly if ever at all. The answer to these questions died when he did many years ago. I really don't know the truth of this question. I only recognize the double standard.

# 7. SHAME OF FAMILY, A LEGACY WE SHARED

Ashamed of his own family he was unaware I was ashamed of mine for the same reasons. In his letters he instructs my mother to go meet his parents at a prescribed time. He specifically tells her to go alone, don't stay more than an hour and if asked, say she is Catholic. He hated the way his parents lived. Once when I was working for a real estate developer I needed a ride home to pick up some hand tools. I asked the man to wait in the car and I would run in the garage and get them. As we drove away I noticed my father had come out on the porch to get a look at who I was with. Half drunk and on his day off from the refinery, he couldn't be bothered with coming out to meet him when there was time. It was just as well because I hated the way my parents lived. Just like my father.

My shame of family extends to more than my parents. I never expected any one of my siblings to make me proud. But shame of certain family members is earned not bestowed. I had a teacher in high school who gave everyone an 'A' the first day of class. Then he said everything you do from now till the end of the term either supports that grade or takes away from it. In this way I have not been able to support the good reports of certain family members still alive today. They have simply pissed me off over and over until there grades are less than passing. I have been more than charitable to some of them; acts that were never acknowledged or returned. I don't like the way they live, how they act, what they say to me and behind my back. Their failure to embrace accountability seals my mind to forgiveness. With these attitudes I have become my father incarnate.

# 8. Misanthropic contempt of others

My father was always critical, hateful and belligerent when he was drunk. The world and the people in it were mindless, contemptuous baggage taking up too much space with their needs and desires. I learned to be this way as well until I realized I was one of the people I despised. That was a revelation I could have lived without. But it is a sad tragic truth of the legacy I adopted exclusively from my father. Self deprecation and self loathing coupled with an inherent hatred of all that is not directly under my control. In the legacy, people outside the dysfunctional core are only reported to be real and have no claim to substantial relevance or impact on members of the core. An outsider's qualitative impressive intellection would have no meaning and their opinions and existence were partially if not fully denied, unless of course there was something to be gained by it.

## 9. UNREASONABLE DEMANDS OF FAMILY, UNUSUAL ACCEPTANCE OF OTHERS

Always down on us, always kind to others. It is a function of the alcoholic legacy to push the abusive envelope of inclusion to whoever would stand for it and not bolt away. Family members are captives and never escape until they are physically removed from the situation. Then other problems can occur. Close friends and loved ones can also become included until they stray from the pack. My parents had few friends. There were some long time acquaintances we saw perhaps once a year or less. The other people were "Christmas card" friends they had met during the war or their ill fated move to Australia.

Some of these friends had histories that needed to be repeated over and over to insure their status stayed beneath my parents. As an example my parents had some friends from the shipyards, Paul and Margie. When their name came up my mother would comment "Margie's daughter was PG", (a code for pregnant). For forty years when Margie's name came up the comment "her daughter was PG", came up with it. I think now these people couldn't stand to be around my parents for very long and saw through their very transparent shield of politeness. Old friends consequently made short visits on certain occasions and only as a courtesy to my parents; a practice made possible by a long forgotten code of proper manners.

In spite of all the back stabbing and abuse, my father would extend kindness to people he didn't even know. He would yell at us in the car for no reason then pull over to pick up a stranded trucker, share his cigarettes and carry on a lively conversation with him as though nothing had happened. If he saw a drunk stumbling down the sidewalk he would offer him a ride home. Once we had gone to see my father's aunt Leota in what was then called, "the rest home". On the return trip with me in the back seat he picked up a drunk who didn't know where he lived. We drove around this particular town for about an hour hoping this drunk would recognize some familiar feature near his home. He never did. He shortly thereafter vomited on the floor of the front seat. My father had all he could do to get this shit faced drunk out of the car and put him on a park bench in the shade. We had to drive about 15 miles to get home and it was a very hot day. The stench of the alcohol and vomit was incredible. My father commented to me, "he didn't want to go home anyway", as an excuse for not completing the mission of delivering him home, like he needed an excuse. The car smelled like puke for years.

## 10. Unnecessary cruelty as retribution

It was beatings, emotional abuse, verbal abuse, degradation, humiliation, and then the silent treatment. I learned to hate all this in my father and I later recognized I was capable of it myself. Because of this revelation I launched full speed into the next item, denial. It is really hard to own up to your bullshit when you have been abused and need to be validated for who you are inside and removed from the faults you are accused of; which can be totally different from the faults you are actually guilty of. The validation for one's feelings is an acceptable and necessary part of humanity. However, when another's needs are being denied and when cruelty and abuse are added as an extension for lack of validation, hostility and hatred emerge as immeasurable rage. Often this paradigm plays out as reprisal for the intense anger generated over very small conflicts. When I was cruel to others I incorrectly validated myself for my assumed correct actions. It all amounted to nothing more than denial.

# 11. DENIAL, DENIAL, DENIAL

The legacy is very much about denial. All bad behavior is denied, accountability forgotten, and truth becomes a fictional character to be despised. The rules of denial say; I can do it if someone else did it. Never tell the full truth if you don't need to. Act smart when it makes you look good, act stupid when it serves you as well. See only what pleases you; be blind to everything else, especially bad behavior. And most importantly the belief that, "I don't have a problem, everyone else does". If my father had lived to this day he would see some of his grandchildren spend time in jail. There was one in San Quentin for charges related to an armed robbery. Another picked up as a teenager for drunk driving. There is at least one of them still suffering in the battle with substance abuse. Behavior my father would have found despicable in others and offences he surely would have deprecated.

Yet I believe the legacy of denial created the avenue for these children to go astray. Every car accident they had was someone else's fault; every time their house was robbed it was done by people outside their sphere of friends even though one of the children had a problem with methamphetamine. Their parents constantly made excuses for them even after conviction and incarceration. When my mother went into the hospital to die one brother told me his son was living with his friends somewhere. Supposedly no one knew where. The truth; he was in the county jail awaiting trial for several felony offences. The same brother told his daughter that my mother was getting better everyday she was in the hospital. The truth; she was given a prognosis of immediate death save for the respirator she was on. After my mother's death this particular daughter called me one day because she was so upset her parents had lied to her. She couldn't have known my parents had lied to me as well and I didn't tell her. I watched with some amazement as my brother and his wife espoused a mediocre form of pretzel logic to explain all the short comings of their children and of themselves. I would have respected them much more if one of them at anytime had stood up and simply said "I fucked up".

# 12. PLAYING FAVORITES AS A MANIPULATION OF THE CHILDREN

My father liked giving rewards to the sibling having children for creating his ideal family unit. Denying help was a transparent manipulation of those living outside the box and was punishment for refusing to buy the acceptable behavior of marriage and breeding. At some point I realized these were among the reasons I never had children of my own. It wasn't as if all his grandchildren really pleased him or loved him in anyway. Some of them were hardly affected at all when one of my brothers waited several days to tell them he had died. They saw him so little they thought he was dead already even though at the time they lived only 2 doors away on the same street as my parents.

My brother bought a book about dying from the Christian book store, read it to the kids and then told them grandpa was dead. He couldn't explain it himself. His wife wanted nothing to do with the task. At the funeral she wouldn't even enter the room where the body was because it gave her "nightmares". Perhaps there was some guilt at work. Anyway, the grandchildren went off and played normally unaffected by the news.

# 13. THE LONER, A CONVENIENT VICTIM

If we were to believe the letters and the subsequent life led by this man it would go something like this: "Nobody knows the trouble I've seen, but let me tell you about it anyway. Nobody's wife is fatter, nobody's children are more ungrateful, nobody's job pays less, nobody's health is worse, nobody is more alone and nobody needs to drink more than me. But it is not my fault, oh, no I never did anything to cause this, it was all put on me by others."

I always felt sorry for my father. He never had any friends he could just get in the car with and go somewhere. In the letters he never mentions his friends by name. Maybe he didn't make any friends. If he did they didn't follow him home. When I was growing up he never bought himself any clothes except when he absolutely needed them. Once my mother bought him a nice gray tweed coat for his birthday, another time he got a Hawaiian shirt. He would wear them together, the tweed coat over the bright blue colored shirt. Although I can't fault his fashion sense he could have listened to someone tell him they did not really go together. But the tragedy is no one ever did. Too afraid I guess. Maybe we just didn't care what he looked like. If we did we wouldn't have let him go out in that powder blue leisure suit. At least he never wore jumpsuits that were popular then. When he died we made sure he wore a proper shirt and tie to match his coat.

On his day off he would sometimes leave the house alone and go to the movies. I never understood this as I am sure my mother liked going to the movies. Middle of the day he would just go and later he would take himself to dinner at The New Roundup Restaurant, a western rodeo themed greasy spoon. He would sit alone and have dinner. He would have spaghetti and meatballs with garlic bread. I guess he liked doing the dinner and a movie thing but he always liked to do it alone. Such activities depressed me so much I have never in my life gone to the movies alone. I have wanted to at times but this part of the history is currently untouchable. It's a simple thing but it reminds me so much of how my father acted I have never done it. In his letters he would take leave from the army alone claiming it was easier for one guy to hitch a ride than two or more. The truth is he was just a loner.

# 14. THE PARADOX, DO AS I SAY NOT AS I DO

If I acted like my father did I would be arrested, lose my children and spend time in jail. Take all the behavior, the drinking, the abuse, even the dead end job he had and he would talk about what kind of loser would do these things never looking in the mirror at himself. Socrates said, "The unexamined life is not worth living". He may have been talking about my father save that Socrates died a couple of thousand years before. The letters reveal a hint of an internal struggle but mostly they put the struggle outside and onto other people. It was always ultimately others at fault not him. If not for his devotion to the Catholic Church there would be no surrender to authority at all. However, even in that religious piety there were loopholes in the devotion. It is sometimes said "a pious fraud is still first cousin to a miracle", so therein he believed he was devout. Or so it seemed.

The letters reveal a typical pattern repeated by all successive generations of alcoholics. Many of the obvious roles and behavioral patterns delineated in the multi generation alcoholic legacy are clearly exhibited in these documents. The destructive legacy must be broken and a new identity discovered to avoid the behavior of the abuser and the adoption of those personality traits as acceptable. I know, I've been there, on both sides of the coin.

The letters towards the end find my father in an army hospital. First in some undisclosed location in the south pacific then in Colorado where his parents lived after his grandfather died. The letters are full of rage and anger towards the system, the government, the army, my mother and everyone else. It was always said that he got a medical discharge but after my mother's death we found two different discharge papers. One that said discharge was because of an ear infection and another claimed discharge due to ear infection and nervous disorder. "Shell shock" was a more common term for people coming apart because of the action but I think my father's disorder was at the time indefinable. He never actually saw any combat. It was the end of the war anyway. They just let him go at that. Clearly the discharge papers deleting the nervous disorder were either forged or obtained in some way to insure he could find work. Another dirty little secret unearthed after the fact. What will I find in the future?

# What Is My Legacy?

As you could imagine, I began to develop some real ambivalent feelings about life and my role in it. My connection with the higher force quietly demanded that I produce something of value in this life. I do not think this pig in my head is a result of abuse and constant need to please but a reaction to those who have wasted the life they have been given. I have had an abundance of this type of role model in my life.

It is always nice to have material things, even flaunt them if you have struggled to earn them. But such a desire to produce an enduring personal legacy transcends the need for material things. At the same time it engenders change for the material world. Beyond a need for self actualization, the desire to leave this world some positive enduring legacy is different. A sort of paradox where need and necessity follow parallel but juxtaposed routes. Indeed many people have gone to the nut house trying to figure out what this means for them personally. Anyone who sincerely struggles with this elusive ideal knows what it is to bay like a hound outside the walls of the asylum. They feel pressure to create positive changes that are lasting but are paralyzed by the options in life. It's like being in a boat in a storm when you have charts, your compass works but all is useless because of the immensity of the waves. Such is the life of those who painfully seek what they cannot see nor understand.

Leaving a personal legacy for the world is a project few set out to accomplish consciously and deliberately. Whether the legacy is positive or negative it is often not intended and not often conceived nor sculpted by precise action. The writings of great authors are many times just a piece of a large uninteresting body of work. The actions of great heroes are done in situations they are thrust into and not often chosen. The doors to great discoveries and research are often accidentally found and built on from there. It is sometimes considered virtuous for an individual to want or need to leave a positive personal legacy. Regardless of intention or deliberate action the fruit of such endeavors are often not realized in that person's lifetime. And very often noted only shortly after their death. I remember something the great jazz musician Charles Mingus had to say on the subject. At a concert in San Francisco he stepped up to the microphone and said, "now when I die I know you're gonna run out and buy my records. That don't do me any good now".

So is it financial reward I seek or recognition for my diligence? Well, both and other things too. Mostly it is the unidentifiable other things that haunt me in my hours of anxiety. Questions mostly, things like, how can I be accountable for all the things I have done and pass on some good ideals from the lesson? Is there a greater purpose in life than to be broken by my past and driven to break others. Can I overcome the pain of my past memories without bonding comfortably to denial? Shall I be of the world or merely in it? What is my purpose? What shall I leave when I am gone; the map, the road or the gold mine, all three or none? Illusive questions for an uncertain future, mixed with desire and ability make for a confusing and tempestuous internal emotional debate on possible actions. I often just sit still while my head spins.

# PART III

# *Promise of a Bright Future*

Although chaos abounded, alcohol was not always a problem in our house. My father started drinking in earnest when I was about nine years old. Although a great range of abuses occurred prior to that time they were motivated by the alcoholic legacy left to my father from his parents. My father's alcoholism compounded the problems at home and sealed his fate for the rest of his short life. He never returned to who he was before, not that he was a great role model in that either. He never sought nor achieved any sort of recovery. I know the desperation of his wasted life haunted him even though he would deny it.

I remember those early years of my life were a time filled with promise and I thrived in school and creatively. The world seemed to me to be a sort of wonderland where everything was possible. I developed a strong sense of personal command although it may have been limited to being able to ride my bike very fast down the hill near our house. Everything seemed within reach until the darkness closed in. Then my life was like being inside an old darkened barn seeing the light steaming through the boards. It was a certain security although more like being in a prison. I did not understand the changes that were happening as a result of my father drinking.

There were a lot of kids in our neighborhood. I remember great games of hide and seek that involved at least a dozen kids at any given time. We hung out together often and roamed the streets as one large benign gang. The train tracks that led to the Concord Naval Weapons Station were down at the end of the block. Twice a day trainloads of ammunition and bombs would go by to stock the troops in Vietnam. We would stand and watch the trains go by and wondered if there were bombs or guns in the box cars. Sailors and Marines on leave would constantly be hitching rides up and down the highway next to the tracks to go down town. Because of our exposure to the military we would often play army in and around the area that included a creek some blocks away near the intermediate school. Nobody wanted to be the Nazis or the Japs so we all fought on one side against imaginary enemies. We never lost and it made for some great war games and we were all promoted and made heroes at one time or another.

We had great fun with this until some of our brothers and their friends had to actually face the draft. They went away and some of them never came back. Then no one wanted to play army anymore. I remember one guy from the local high school. A football star, he enjoyed wearing and showing off his varsity letter sweater. He would walk by our house with his handful of books on his way to and from school. When it was his turn to go he gallantly went off to Vietnam. When he came home he would occasionally wander by our house, his blank stare always straight ahead. As before he wore that same letter sweater he was so proud of. He walked the streets for several years until his brightly colored letter sweater was a shredded rag hanging from his body. Instead of books he carried a garbage bag half full of something unknown. He later just vanished from sight, a homeless casualty of war. Since Vietnam playing army is not as popular as it once was.

I did have many good times as a child. Not all my years were spent in constant turmoil. In the early years I couldn't fully intellectualize what was going on. I just tried to be a kid. When I was 12 I got an Oakland Tribune paper route. I was pretty good at delivering papers but not so good at collecting the money. People always dodged me and I feared complaints from cutting them off as they counted against the points I received. Still I did well and was often rewarded with tickets to sports events for gaining points from new subscriptions. My favorites were baseball tickets. It was always the Giants against the Dodgers, a great 1960's rivalry. Those were the days when Willie Mays and Don Drysdale played. There were so many players who became legendary I am now sorry I didn't take more notice of the history involved. I even had a number 24 Giants jersey, Willie Mays' number. I loved that shirt. Willie McCovey, Jesus Alou, Orlando Cepada and all the great ball players of the time. The Giants were my team. I was there and it was like magic. I still wear a black and orange Giant's cap today.

Delivering papers was a real hassle sometimes but I persevered. The Sunday edition was a morning paper. I had to be at the paper shack at 5:00 A.M. to put in the inserts, fold and deliver the papers. It was always dark and very often cold. I fondly remember the image of all of us boys gathered around a fire we had going in a 55 gallon drum outside the shack. Fueled by the previous days papers it smoked like mad and you had to know just what distance to stand from it to stay warm and not die of smoke inhalation. As a prank sometimes a boy would toss a handful of rubber bands in the fire and stink everyone out. Soon enough though the manager would show up, let us in and then the paper truck would come. It was time to get on with the job. We folded our papers and scattered across our section of the city to deliver them.

Sometimes we finished early and met up at the school for the prank of the day. Williams Elementary School was the site of many pranks. Sometimes we would raise a garbage can up the flag pole. One time we borrowed a bicycle from a sleeping school mate and put it up there as well. My personal favorite was dumping a bottle of dish soap in the fountain at the hospital a few blocks away. That had to be done in the very early morning before the papers were delivered to give it enough time to agitate. By the time we rode by to go to church the suds were mile high. It was great.

Most of the paper boys were Catholic so we tried to finish our routes and get to early mass at 8:00 A.M. to get it out of the way. We were a sight to see. A rag tag bunch of boys sitting together, our hands filthy from the news print, our faces smudged by the soot of the paper fire. Often bundled against the cold, we would wear our gloves in church to hide our dirty hands and the nuns would stare at us with evil faces. We would talk and joke and try to get someone to laugh out loud. Sometimes the nuns, who always took up the first two rows on the right side, made us sit with them so we wouldn't talk. There we sat, all the paper boys with one penguin between each of us. Sometimes that made it harder not to laugh. After mass we would escape through the side door and run to the pile of beat up bikes locked together as one. Then we were off our separate ways home for breakfast.

Most of the boys had two bikes. One beat up bike with a special rack for the paper route and a shiny Schwinn ten speed they bought with the money from delivering papers. I remember when I had saved the $85.00 necessary to buy mine. I was really excited. Everybody chose a different color and I chose the blue one. It was 1968 and there were some new features such as shifters on the handle bars instead of down below. It was a great bike and beautiful as well. I bought a generator light and a small rack for it. I put hundreds of miles on it and I still own it today. It is in good working order after 34 years. It was an important moment in my life and I have always treasured it. It was my pay off and my escape for many years. I expected life to be much the same way with simple work and a big pay off. I was a little naive.

# The Good Years

A bout this time my paternal grandfather died. I met him only three times that I can remember. I was young and one of my only memories of him was that he was very tall with pure white hair. My father's mother, my grandmother, came from Denver and as I previously mentioned lived in our house for many years. Born in 1883, she was a bigoted racist from an Irish, Arkansas family. Eighty-three years old, nearly totally deaf, and suffering from senile dementia, she descended onto our house. Replete with incontinence, and the unmistakable odor of an old lady who wore a black wool dress even on the hottest days of the year and bathed only once a week. She clomped around on the hardwood floors of the house like an animal with cloven hooves, farting and sometimes urinating as she passed by. If you saw this scene in a movie you would say it could never happen, but it did. It happened to us. I often remember standing around shaking my head at the sight. I watched in astonishment as she began to affect everything that went on in the house.

She was a crazy old woman who thought tangerine Life Savers were her medicine. Since she was on Medicare, she thought medicine was free. She would go down to the corner store and scoop up several rolls and put them in her pocket and walk out. The store owner was sterling about it and would just call our house. He would tell my father what happened. My father would then go into her drawer and count the rolls then send one of us to the store to pay for them. Sometimes she would not return from her trips to the store because she had either gone into the neighbors home by mistake while they were gone (doors were rarely locked in those days) or walked past our house and become lost somewhere down the street or around the corner. I remember my father, upon seeing my grandmother pass our house at full speed, telling me to go get her and bring her home.

We referred to her as old grandma since my mother's mother was about 15 years younger. Old grandma would retire to her room at night and turn on this hand held transistor radio full blast on a preset station and hold it to her good ear. She thought the doctor had told her that it would cure her hearing problem and each night for about an hour this noise would emanate from her room. It is doubtful she could hear it at all since she could barely hear her own hearing aids whistling. As children we would often sneak up on her from behind and whistle really loud to see if we could get a reaction from her. Sometimes she would immediately grab at her hearing aids and try to adjust them which started them to whistle in earnest. It was a small prank but offered great laughs when successful.

Every so often about eleven or twelve at night old grandma would appear fully dressed and ready for the day's worth of sitting on the couch. We would have to take her to the door and open it to show her it was night time and tell her she should go back to bed. She would say "well I'll be" and return to her room. She lived to be over one hundred years old and died two weeks after my father.

I was much older when I found out her dementia was caused by years of alcohol abuse. It was commonly called "wet brain" in those days. Little was ever said about her past or my father's history of growing up. It was as though everything that happened before she moved in didn't happen or as if she just appeared out of nowhere. Living in an extended family household is very stressful for everyone. But the added secrets didn't make for good intrigue, just more denial and anger.

# Better Days, Better Role Models

My mother's parents came to America from a small island in Norway called Aalesund. It is a magical place I have visited as an adult. I was a small child when I noticed one day my grandparents spoke English with accents. They would often correct each others English and then laugh about it. They lived in Fort Bragg, California during its day as a logging town and fishing village. Their house, really a shack, was about a mile outside of town on a small piece of land in the redwoods; small in size but big on adventure as a kid. Spending a couple of weeks there in the summer was really a high point for me in my life. The small coastal town was cool in the summer unlike the city. The people, the fishing, exploring the woods and trips to the beach were great fun. There was some high adventure nearly every day. It felt good to be exploring another world where people lived so differently.

For many years as a small boy I would often ask my grandfather to take me out salmon fishing on the boat he kept at the harbor. He would tell me I wasn't old enough but, when I was, I could feed the crabs when we go out. We spent some of our time on the docks jigging for herring in the evening when they came in to the harbor. Herring were best caught just before and right after sunset. The jig had six hooks on it and there were so many herring you could sometimes bring in one on every hook. We would always catch a bucket full. There were always a lot of people jigging for herring in the evening. My grandfather would go up and down the dock and trade the large fish we caught for smaller ones that were more the size needed for salmon fishing. An entire fish was used on each line for bait. Today the herring no longer come into Noyo Harbor.

The day finally came when one of my brothers and I were old enough. We got up early and got down to the boat. Out to sea we went expecting great adventure and excitement. Suddenly we were both sea sick and vomiting over the side of the boat. As we barfed my grandfather said "that's it boys, feed the crabs". So that's what he meant. On successive trips I overcame my sea sickness and really began to enjoy my time on the ocean. We caught all manner of fish, salmon, red snapper, flounder and occasionally a shark.

My first shark experience was memorable. A small shark got onto one of the lines and he was brought on board as he was tangling all the other lines. My grandfather's boat partner gaffed it through the snout upside down on the wooden deck and my grandfather held its tail. With its teeth bulging out and its body thrashing around my grandfather tossed a knife down on the deck and told me to cut open his gut. I grabbed the knife and stabbed it several times but could not penetrate the skin. Everyone was laughing at me because he had tossed me a dull butter knife as a joke. There is no way to cut shark skin with anything but a very pointed sharp knife.

Grandpa's partner, a Scotsman named Fay McBride finished the job with a puka knife and the carcass was thrown overboard, all the while everyone was laughing. We left the area and fished some distance away. As the day wore on the shark seemed to grow in size in everyone's memory. By the time we got home it was enormous. I learn two things that day. I needed a good knife and how fish stories get started. My times on the boat were memorable and far removed from my world at home. I caught many large fish over the years and I actually brought some home to prove it.

My grandfather was fearless on the ocean. He had gone to sea as a boy of 13 (about 1912) sailing from Norway to far away places and back on a sailing ship. As a Norwegian he was born to the ocean. On his own boat, many decades later, he could navigate by some sort of dead reckoning. I only saw him sincerely use the compass on one occasion in the fog. We always wore life jackets as kids but later left them in the hold. I became fearless of the sea as well although 15 foot swells often scared me to death. At least I didn't barf anymore.

There was only one time I saw my grandfather terrified. We were visiting them as usual in the summer but stayed behind to go to the beach. He came home from fishing alone that day as white as a ghost. He began to spin a yarn about a giant octopus that had attacked his boat and he had to fight for his life. He and the boat were nearly lost in the struggle. We didn't believe him. We thought he had one too many drinks at Mary Milano's Bar after fishing. The next day he was in no hurry, no desire really to go fishing. We went down to the dock with him later that day and to our amazement there were large round pieces of paint missing from all over the boat. It looked as if rows of tentacles had stripped the boat of its paint in these areas. We know today that giant squid sometimes attack boats. Since he never saw its head he didn't know what it was, just another sea monster. He was visibly shaken though for sometime to come.

My grandmother Caspara was a small, kindly Norwegian jewel. Nothing really surprised her about Grandpa's adventures. They had been sweethearts and together since they were small children. They knew each other for all their lives. Aalesund is a small island about one third the way up Norway's west coast. My grandfather came to America on one of his sailing trips and sometime later sent the money for her to come as well. From this love affair comes a typical 1920 Ellis Island story of the new bride to be waiting for the groom who is still out at sea. She was retrieved from the island by a Danish woman who shared the same last name as my grandfather and whose son was his friend. Soon he returned and they were married and their long American adventure began.

I always liked my Norwegian grandparents as they were so very different from other people in our family. Grandma kept house and was active at the Moose lodge and the Sons of Norway. She wrote in a diary for every day since 1935. When she died I was able to find all her diaries from 1953 to one day before she died in 1984. I had a special bond with her as she was my caretaker immediately after I was born. My mother was too ill from the difficult birth to come home for many weeks. My grandmother took care of me for those weeks. All these events are recorded in her diaries.

She called me one day and wanted to see me the next Saturday. She said over the phone she didn't know if she would see me again. I thought it was a strange thing to say but since she recently had a small stroke coupled with her age and ever present Norwegian accent things didn't always come out right. She was terribly lonely as my grandfather had died some years before. She cried everyday because she missed him so much I believe she died of a broken heart. On our last outing to breakfast she told me she had a dream that grandpa was waiting for her. He looked young like he did when they first came to America. She asked me what it meant. I told her he was watching over her. But I knew it meant she would soon join him. And she did, late the next day. I was the last one to see her alive.

They were a funny couple together. He too would like a drink after work and then he would get mushy on her, kissing her cheeks and all. She would always bring him sandwiches and whatever he wanted. When he came home he would always find a flower for her somewhere on the property. After he died she brought him a flower everyday, to his picture on the bookcase.

Most of the year when it was not salmon season my grandfather painted houses and businesses. My grandmother liked to drive us through town and point out the houses and say "daddy painted this house" or "grandpa is going to paint this store". When he died we were sitting in the family section of the funeral home. She was teary and distraught. She was gazing around the room when a smile came over her face. She turned to me and said, "Daddy painted this place too".

My wife and I often return to the coast for vacation and hope to live there someday. Days and nights by the sea calm me and help me remember a softer past and to dream of a brighter future. I have no desire to become a surf bum or salty sailor. I would simply rather live where nature helps you decide how you live your life. Where not everything is paved and concreted over. Where hard lines are softened and absolutes can blow away with the wind or melt in the salt air. This is my dream of the future now and how long it has been in coming. The danger created by the alcoholic legacy is never forgotten. But a few good role models in life bring back some of the pieces of the puzzle as I have tried to reassemble my life. I now seek this reformation through cathartic writing and regular visits with a great counselor; Gail, the architect of my recovery.

# Here and Now

Out of necessity I got involved in the construction business many years ago. I actually started with a job watering plants and picking up garbage at some shopping centers. There was an annex being built next to one of the centers. One day the contractor was short handed and asked if I knew how to hammer nails. I said yes and rarely picked up garbage after that. I did my apprenticeship as a carpenter and branched out into the other trades.

I became a general contractor about 20 years ago and have performed as an expert witness in litigation, an industry expert for the Contractors State License Board and became an arbitrator in 1992. Because of my issues with accountability I developed an intense dislike for some lawyers and have since stopped arbitrating and no longer work as a witness or as an industry expert. My days are sometimes spent wondering why I am still a contractor too. I have developed an excellent client base and I have not had the need to advertise in over ten years. Although work is sometimes slow I am eventually called and suddenly too busy. I'll never get used to it and someday hope to exit this business for more a cerebral pursuit and work that is important and not so very urgent.

The work itself is emotionally unfulfilling and mentally stressful not to mention hard on me physically. After my last knee surgery, it was nearly impossible to return to work after the prescribed recovery period. Nothing new ever happens and the most litigious business in the country gets more expensive to maintain as the years go by.

Also lost in the years have been many friends and coworkers to death. Recently my long time friend and tax accountant Paul died suddenly from a heart attack. Having grown up in the construction business I watched as many of the older journeymen who taught me the carpentry trade retired and died. Some of the younger guys more my age have died as well in recent years from heart attacks, drug overdoses, cancer, AIDS and accidents. Only one of the true old timers is still alive; old Lou. I see him in church occasionally (because I only go occasionally) and I hope he lives to see 100. As for me, now I am one of the gray beards everyone talks about. When I was younger I never thought I would be this old and still in this business. Now that I am here I find it harder to adapt to the changing work environment with the huge influx of cheap labor that out bids me on a regular basis. I still enjoy the carpentry work and finer finishing jobs such as kitchens but my days in the business are numbered. I only hope I get to pick the number and not be at the mercy of some accident or the predicted failure of my natural knee joint damaged in two previous accidents. All I can say is "I'm working on it".

Always in my mind is this question of the legacy. The important thing I will leave this world. I am often full of advice and could fill volumes. But I know this thing I must do is for me not others. Although others may benefit from it, the passage is mine and the quality of my life's contribution will be a reflection of my inner self and strength. Acquired inner wisdom is sometimes intangible and unexplainable and therefore impossible to share. At this point I would say if you know what I mean, no explanation is necessary. If you don't know what I mean no explanation is possible.

To use the cliché "hope springs eternal" would best describe where I am, where I have been and where I want to go. When one grows up as I did with mixed values and diverse and damaged role models, there can be some intellectual confusion, some physical degradation and some spiritual deficits to overcome. Yet there is always a need to continue, a reason to survive. An instinct or a desire I am not sure which. I look again to my past for the answers.

# Back To The Past

When I was seven years old I woke up one night suffocating. I was in complete respiratory failure. My parents rushed me to the hospital but I was already blue in the face, my tongue swollen and black. Before I passed out the doctors were trying to shove an airway down my throat. The last thing I heard was "we're losing him". I went to sleep and had the strangest dream of going towards this light. There were people there who were kind but I was not allowed to pass beyond them. The vision faded and all was suddenly black for the longest time.

I woke up in a hospital bed in a darkened ward with this tube in my throat. I choked and gagged on it for many days and after much struggling it was removed and I could breathe on my own again. I was inside a very crude oxygen tent with plastic all around. My father was in the room with me and seemed more worried than I had ever seen him. The doctors seemed baffled by what had happened to me as there was no underlying infection or asthma. No reason for suffocating as I did. They just shook there heads and told me I could go home when my blackened fingernails showed some pink. I spent many weeks in the hospital recovering. My only friend at this time was a toy kaleidoscope my mother had bought me. It brought me a world of ever changing colors and shapes at a time when my own world had come to a stand-still. Its beauty reminded me of the place I had visited briefly before being brought back to life. I fumbled with the different attachments and was constantly vigilant over my black fingernails hoping and praying some morning I would wake up and they would be normal again. Eventually, a small pink crescent appeared at the cuticle and I was allowed to go home. In later years I would have the recurring nightmare of the incident, sometimes waking in the dream to see one of my brothers standing next to the bed with a pillow in his hand.

The so called near death experience is a hard thing to manage. I think people who hear of it can intellectualize the experience rather well and accept or reject it. Some who experience it find greater meaning to life and indeed find God where there was none before. Some people like me struggle with it and deny it happened and yet we move ahead, our will to survive even greater than one can imagine. With this greater will to live comes a parallel disintegrated fear of death. I no longer fear death as unknown. I have no desire to die but I have no fear of going to the better place. The problem is simply now what do I do with the life I have been given back. I believe I was sent back for a reason. I have struggled to find it ever since. Since my near death experience happened before I experienced the more terrible things in life I have been at a loss to put it into a chronological perspective. It was suggested to me that it was just one more bad thing that happened to me. Yet the lasting memory of what lies just on the other side of life is a constant reminder to push ahead constructively with what little time I have left.

# *Look Within*

Through the dark despair surrounding my childhood I persevered. I tried to find a home in my heart for forgiveness, a place for dreams and a road to follow. Always with me but not readily evident was hope. Blindly moving ahead into later years, I finally distanced myself from the people who hurt and confused me. I graduated with honors from St. Mary's College after thirteen years of night and weekend classes. A great triumph of the spirit for me. I bought a house when I was only 26 years old. I tried to just move ahead at all costs and all situations.

Still with all my small triumphs I must report I have failed at nearly every personal relationship I have had with the opposite sex. Until recently I formed long lasting relationships with only a few guys I know. I have one from my early childhood, one from high school and one from my substance abusing days. (Or should I say daze). We remain in contact for several reasons and although I share something in common with each of them, they have nothing in common with each other. My friend Jimmy from early childhood flies an airliner for United. My friend Ken from high school operates a water treatment plant for a city nearby. Michael now works for a software company and diligently works with Alcoholics Anonymous. Guys often overlook each others faults and tend not to blame each other for issues that arise in relationships. This could be because of fear of confrontation or fear of intimacy. It could also be we often say "what the fuck" and let it go, whatever it is. That never seems to happen in male/female relationships.

Remember, it is part of the legacy of alcohol to either blame someone for your problems or be the victim. The sphere of personal relationships is prime breeding ground to act out previously repressed anger and victimization of either yourself or others. In the legacy paradigm, trust is shattered into so many pieces; intimate personal relationships are often doomed from the start. Add to it the problem of choosing the wrong person with the same or conflicting issues and there is no chance for a smooth transition from dating to long term bliss. In the sphere of male female relationships I have been accused of being difficult to live with, a liar, self centered, egotistic, misogynistic, cruel, careless, unfeeling, unthinking, irresponsible; incapable of being present, intimate, sharing, thoughtful, fair or trustworthy. At one time or another I have been guilty of all these things and carry some shame from this personal revelation.

I feel bad for all the trouble I have caused to unsuspecting partners but I was helpless to act in any other way. I have genuinely hated myself for these broken relationships and the damage I caused to decent people. I also recognize some of my own shattered dreams in the debris left behind. In my own role as abuser I lost the good parts of myself to the legacy that defined me for so many years. I had always hoped that I would someday be different. Through the love and compassion of a good lady I am finally coming to a place where I might find the resolve to resurrect my spirit again anew.

Other than my wife Kathie, all my romantic relationships ended shattered into pieces. Kathie is the only women with the kindness and monumental patience to not only put up with my surly nature but inspire me to seek outside help for my problems. For this and other reasons I can say I have never loved any one as much as Kathie nor as well as Kathie. She is a great gift to me from God. I hope someday I can be as good for her as she has been for me. For seven years now we continue to live together with each others faults and blessings. Success is found partly in our devotion to stay together and the commitment of being decent to each other. It is not an easy task for either of us or for anyone in relationship. Trust is the key. I trust she will never leave me nor do anything to damage what we have. She trusts me in the same way. Trust is not something you have in an alcoholic household. It is earned and learned only through honesty and accountability.

Finally, I found a counselor to help me sort out my feelings. My feelings are something I may talk a lot about but sometimes avoid saying anything meaningful. Working with the diagnosis of Post Traumatic Stress Disorder seems to help unify my fragmented emotions and smooth out the jagged mental state that brings me to anger so quickly. I can say now I am no longer an angry man. I just get a little mad sometimes. The answer is in standing still from time to time. Taking no action save to observe myself and how I feel. Not to react, just make note. Unload the emotion and give myself some forgiveness. Maybe later say I'm sorry for what I have done or said. Maybe surrender before the fight. I now have a few options for a new era in my life.

I am now some years into this process of emotional recovery and it will continue for some time to come. I consider myself lucky to have come so far in resolving some of these issues. Not without considerable help from my counselor Gail and not without considerable work on my part. I often consider Gail the architect of my recovery. Her guidance and focus have laid the cornerstone for a new life for me. I've just to finish building it. Writing this book has been a big part of that process. Sometimes raw and unpolished it records my feelings and chronicles the part of my life that became so loosely woven, a tug at a string unraveled the whole fabric. Now with the loose ends being tied up, a new challenge has emerged; what to do with my life now. My old life and all the experiences I've had defined me in every way. What will define me now?

Krishnamurti often said, "Truth is a pathless land". Meaning it is a quality you either possess or not. There is no path to it; it resides in your heart. You just need to find it there. In the Revelation by St. John, there is a similar message. Regarding the arrival of the Kingdom of Heaven, there is much debate in the New Testament about the events and time frame that will lead the main event. This time it is

John who says the Kingdom of Heaven is already here, meaning within your heart.

It would seem that most of the answers we seek are also there in our hearts, waiting, hidden, sometimes driven down but never out of that which is pure within us. There waits the undeniable voice of reason and compassion. This explains many things that occur in our lives, things like making selfless decisions, putting right before wrong and others ahead of ourselves. I hate to say it but I believe people are basically good inside. I hate to say it but I am basically good as well. There I said it.

# I Bury My Parents, I Bury My Past

I believe my mother came to a similar conclusion in the years before she died. She was so controlled by my father when he was alive. When he died one of the first things she did was buy a brand new car. The next thing she did was follow my lead and visit the family she had never met in Norway, an unforgettable place I had traveled to prior to that time. Whereas, most of us thought she would wither away after my father died she actually did the opposite and become more independent. One of the last memories I have of her was watching her look at a small lace and flower center piece for a table she was given by a friend. Nothing terribly special except it was pretty. I noticed how simply delighted she was to turn it and look at it from several angles. It was such a simple thing that brought her so very much pleasure. I felt then that she had somehow been healed herself. She moved on in her way perhaps.

Our last conversation was about our upcoming wedding in a month. She wanted to buy some small cameras to put on all the tables as a present and was thrilled when Kathie and I liked the idea. She was also excited about the wedding of a friend she would attend on that next day which was Saturday. According to her friends she looked better than ever that Saturday and had a great time. Monday brought her to the hospital when her platelets suddenly dropped. She died on Wednesday from complications of diabetes and kidney failure. We had enough warning to be at her side when the end came. It is a great gift to be with someone you love when they pass. Something I can't explain. I know what to expect on the other side so I had no fear for her. However, since then I have been terribly sad to be without her.

The night she died, we went into the house and on the table was the bag of cameras with a note saying what they were for. Also on the chair was another present for us she had just finished wrapping, the scissors laid neatly on top after trimming the ribbon. On the table were birthday cards for everyone still to have birthday that year. She knew it was her time to go and she did what she could to put everything in order. Most of us would be very lucky to have that opportunity. Sometimes the smallest of miracles are the most astonishing; the blessings from the meek the most powerful. I often stand and wonder how these seemingly trivial things carry so much mysticism and generate so much hope. My mother was lucky in the end, my father was not.

In 1977 my father went into the hospital for a bypass operation on his legs. During the procedure it was discovered he had a form of inoperable intestinal cancer. This later spread to his liver and into something called carcinoid syndrome; cancer of the nervous system. He had fought melanoma for years getting chunks of his face cut off at regular intervals but never a word that it might spread to other areas in this way. I can suppose without liability that working at a chemical refinery for twenty-eight years didn't help the situation from progressing. The prognosis was death would occur in two months to two years. Still a valiant battle with chemo therapy and radiation ensued.

My father did not die quickly. His cancer spread, remised and spread again over five years. He was very sick and in great pain most of the time. In the last weeks of his life he went in and out of a comma. A couple of years into all this the doctors said he could die at any time but he didn't. After five years the doctors did not know what kept him alive. I visited him nearly everyday in the final weeks. On one day he was lucid I asked him if he had any pain. He replied "don't worry about me; I'm going to be free. You're the one who has to stay". It was an unexpected acceptance of his death. I was shocked and relieved at the same time. Maybe he was human after all.

This period of my father dying was especially hard for me because I always wanted to get even for all the abusive things he did and said, most of which are not mentioned here. When I was told he was dying, I remember telling my mother I had always wanted him to suffer in some way for his treatment of us but I didn't want this. This cancer thing was not what I had in mind. In later years I realized I blamed myself for his illness and death for having thoughts of getting even somehow. I silently, secretly carried this blame for many years. Fortunately this has passed.

Near the end of his life we were called by the hospital into a family meeting. They wanted to meet soon about his durable power of attorney. We thought it was about pulling the plug but the hospital had another agenda. In that meeting the next day we were informed the insurance company considered my father terminally ill. He was no longer acute because of his durable power of attorney leaving instructions prohibiting heroic life sparing measures upon physical crisis such as a heart attack. The insurance company would no longer pay for this level of treatment. They told us we had three days to move him out of the hospital. They gave us no help or indication where we should move someone on partial life support. Just gave us three days. We were lucky to get him into a convalescent home on the following Monday morning. He died on the next Wednesday at about 12:00 noon. I have often resented the fact they just couldn't wait.

The most interesting thing came out of this. I wasn't able to see him on that Monday but I went to see him on that Tuesday evening. I went into the room he was supposed to be in but his bed was empty. I thought he had died already. I went to the nurse's station and asked about him, if he had died. The nurse said no, he was just at the desk asking for a cigarette and some matches. I informed her that my father had been in a comma for weeks and it was unlikely he walked anywhere on his own. The two nurses looked at each other and immediately sprang into action to find my father or who they thought was my father.

We went down the hall and outside near his room, sitting upright in a chair having a cigarette was my father. I said "Dad, what are you doing". He said, "I'm having a cigarette". We both laughed and he smiled. It occurred to me I hadn't seen him smile for years. My father had this gold tooth just behind his eye tooth. If he smiled in a genuine fashion the gold tooth would show. If he gave a phony smile it would not. As a child I often used it as an indicator to measure if things were really alright or whether he was just putting on a show. On that day the gold tooth shone as brightly as ever. Later my mother and brother came and we sat for a couple of hours talking. Dad finally got into bed and laughed. He didn't understand why he was in bed and we were all sitting around. My mother told him he had been sick. He said he felt fine. He thought he was at home in a hospital bed in the dining room. He also thought we had rented some space to the guy in the bed next to him to bring in extra money.

We didn't tell him he was in a convalescent home. He seemed so cheerful and happy and without pain. It was a miracle we thought, maybe he will get better. He smiled and said good-bye that night as I walked out. Before I could get there the next day he died. Only my mother was with him. I was sad and relieved at the same time. There was finally some peace in his life. All through his long death ordeal he never complained once; never played the victim role. One of the few positive surprises I observed and came to admire in him. His behavior in the death cycle seemed to me like a paradox because the alcoholic legacy left me with black and white vision. No gray and no color. Still there was change. A gift from above maybe, for everyone involved.

My parents are buried next to my sister Kristine whom I never knew. It's ironic they are buried in a pioneer cemetery that dates back to the 1850's. Their old ways of never question, never say, fit quite well with the nearly ancient monuments and fading marble headstones. I have always thought it is a good place for them, a quiet place, even divine. I designed and bought a great granite headstone for all of them. Our family name in a banner across the top.

# *Recovery*

Recovering from your life is not an easy task. First you have to make the commitment to work as long as it takes regardless of the issues that may confine you otherwise. Then you need to start somewhere, recognize milestones along the way for support and guidance, and then figure out when it's finished. Simple, right? Most people probably never attempted it at all. If you are reading this book I can assume you might be one who is looking within. So here's some advice if you are suffering from Post Traumatic Stress Disorder caused by a brutal and violent childhood involving the drug abuse or alcoholism of others. Get some help.

Going to a counselor is a sign of good mental health, not bad. If you suffer from a form of PTSD or any mental or emotional distress, there are problems you are facing you may not understand. There are reasons why you react the way you do; they are not your fault. You cannot intellectualize your feelings; you can only feel them. There are triggers that set you off. There are buttons that push you down. Christmas will always be difficult. Take heart because there are words and medications to help you. Be kind to yourself, seek out some guidance. Do not suffer needlessly. Get some help. Christmas depends on it.

Now having said that let me tell you a little about what my path looked like. First I made the commitment to get some help. This was my hardest step in the beginning stages of my emotional recovery. I had a lot of excuses not to do it for many years but, I became so miserable I needed desperately to feel better on any level.

Then I needed to start somewhere. I took a deep look into my heart and asked myself what it was I really needed. I found out I didn't know. It just hurt there. So I recognized that as the first milestone in a long difficult journey. One that marked the time I saw my confusion for what it was. It was a beast that was indefinable and hard to access mentally and emotionally. It was always with me. In my heart I recognized anger, loss, sadness, anxiety and fear. I didn't see the reason for it; I didn't understand or recognize what triggered it. These emotions permeated my well being and came to define me and my outlook on life. My uncontrollable behavior shattered many relationships and dreams as well. Although outwardly I seemed fine, inside I was crying out for help.

I was rigid in my opinions about insignificant things, overcautious of any activity that might bring anyone such as my wife, step children or friends into danger. I hated crowds at the movies and Christmas. The holidays were terribly stressful for me for no apparent reason. I would say things that I didn't mean or feel were true, especially in anger. Above all I didn't believe I was capable of ever being anything other than what I was; one step short of a loser for not sorting out this inner uncontrollable rage.

Because of this I decided to seek out some counseling again. My nightmares had returned and I would wake up stressed to the max. My nightmares often involved bloody battles with unknown people and creatures and I remember being severely and mortally wounded several times. I have even died in my nightmares. My nightmares were not confusing, just bloody and full of violence. I would wake up thoroughly disturbed which set the tone for a very bad day. However, my bad dreams became a portal to help identify some of the negative thought patterns I unconsciously harbored in my head. Each character in the dream was some aspect of me and each action an indication of my emotional or mental understanding of that aspect. Sounds simple but I am talking about literally hundreds of dreams during several years to puzzle over. It was a big problem and a good place to work from.

I also had the help of medication. I won't go into the roller coaster ride of finding the correct medication or dosage. But, I will say medication has helped me and can be part of the puzzle of recovery. A very small dose of a very mild drug was the answer for me. So don't be afraid of it, take advantage of all your resources if you can.

The first year of counseling was once a week. After starting with my counselor, I was finding it hard to focus on any one incident or problem that superceded any other. My mind was a mash of emotions with no particular event the cause. Some days I was stressed because of current events and sometimes about the past. However, we began by unraveling each issue and event or emotion that brought me to pain or feelings of danger. We didn't work in that order or inclusive of each necessarily. We spent probably the first year on past history and current problems that were coming up and tried to tie them to a common thread. I was always mindful of the aspects of my dreams that signaled detection of new problems or the affirmation one had been resolved. Although I am not a big dream therapy advocate, the interpretation of a dream now and then gave me incredible understanding of my progress or lack of it.

In the second year we met every two weeks and worked on the issues that dealt with constructing a new life and reality using information we gleaned from the past year of work. Blue sky wishes, past and current dreams of the future were all put into the mix. We tried to set a goal for the future; what my life could look like if I wanted. We then tackled each problem that stood in the way or affected progress somehow. I am not there yet but I'm getting close to yet another milestone. I almost know instinctively now when I am about to pass into a better state of mind. However, to add intrigue, I cannot predict what these new feelings or resolution of the past will be. Sometimes I discover a hidden pocket of anger over something long forgotten. I just know somehow I am getting closer.

At the start of the third year, we began to focus on just a couple of issues alone. We have been working on my anxiety about money and how I used the problems with money as a dumping ground for all my other anxieties thereby making the money issue emotionally larger than it should be. Another big issue is my trepidation or hesitation to be successful. Most of my personal problems have disappeared and the nightmares are few and far between. My relationship with Kathie is better and better and I reached several milestones in recovery when I realized I wasn't as angry anymore, even though as I said before, I still get a little mad sometimes.

All through this process I was writing. At first I attempted to write a book called *Letters from My Father*. I still may attempt this someday as there is much to be explored. However, there was too much anger and I couldn't sort it out using the single resource. I began to keep a journal but found it was a record of my nightmares and bloody at that. So I began to write some softer stories for children. Picture book stories about our Cocker Spaniel and what went on in her head entitled *Bubby's Back Yard*. There is a book about a skunk that plagued us on vacation one year called *Skunk in the House*. My favorite is called *My Friend Jimmy*, about young friends and their dreams growing up in a Catholic environment. There are several fictional short stories as well. One day I realized that my heart was a stone sometimes, and one that bled for all that has happened to me. I started writing *My Heart is a Stone That Bleeds*. At one point, thinking I said all there is to say; I copyrighted the title and manuscript at the Library of Congress, a milestone in itself. However, I wasn't done and the book you are reading is about three times longer than originally planned.

*My Heart is a Stone That Bleeds* and *My Friend Jimmy* take place in the same time frame. *My Friend Jimmy* records the activities of a couple of kids in a *Leave it to Beaver* style. All the emotional baggage is dropped and the two kids in the book live their story of friendship and discovery from a child's perspective. It was necessary to write this first book to remember that my childhood wasn't all bad and to use it as a resource for further material in this book.

I began to weave parts of some of these works into the one book you are reading now. Although I excelled at writing in college I found myself without a clear assignment to work from. I found how very difficult it is to be inclusive of all the relevant facts and emotions and still produce a readable document that chronicled the partial history of my life. As an additional task I had to reveal parts of myself and the past I wasn't prepared to reveal. I had to show I had made progress and somehow learned something from all this. I began to develop my own assignment. The book took nearly three years to write. I'm glad there was no due date. Things like this are finished when they are finished.

The process of writing is a difficult one by itself. To use writing as a form of cathartic therapy is more than a challenge. If you add to that the need to focus in on a target market for later publication everything gets a little confusing. My regular trips to see Gail were necessary to sort out the kaleidoscope of ideas and conclusions rolling around in my brain. At several points I gave up on the idea of publication and continued to write for the sake of writing. Through this process I began to shed much of the anger I had accumulated over the years and get a better sense of the gifts I possess.

At each point in the process of writing I reached places where I thought I was done. I only wanted to be done because this project was wearing me out. I was recovering from my past, running a business, writing a book and keeping it all together while making progress in this huge commitment to the task of moving on in my life. Like I said before, medication is a part of the recovery puzzle. Sometimes I think it has been the glue to bind my head together during this process so it doesn't explode.

This kind of recovery takes courage. It takes commitment. And it takes vision. You bring the courage and commitment and find someone else to help you with the vision. Be prepared to spend a couple of years reforming your life from one defined by a long painful past to one where you live a better, sweeter life. In that no one can know where the process of recovery will take you, be mindful of your own gifts as you go. Everyone on this earth has a special gift or talent not shared with anyone else. Try to discover your gift, your reason to be. It may be your gift lives close to the surface and just needs to be brought out. Others need to look to the sky for the lost or undiscovered dream.

Either way you have permission to discover and live your dream and share your special gifts with others. It is your right and no one can take it from you.

I am not sure where the end of recovery is for me. It seems that I am far from it sometimes. But I continue. I like my life more now. I stress less about things beyond my control. I am able to rest in my head sometimes. Going to a crowded movie theater is still a challenge but after the movie I realize it was worth it. Some movies are worth it anyway.

Last I would say a person in recovery needs to define his/her support group. Who is in your life that supports what you are attempting to do? Are they friends, family or members of an organization specifically tailored for your needs? Do you have a counselor you resonate with? One who stands outside you and tells you the truth regardless of how harsh it may sound. You will need support and it is a sign of good mental health to seek them out when you need them. Emotional recovery doesn't involve forgetting the past, it involves resolving the past. It can take a long time so pace yourself. And most of all prepare yourself for some unexpected changes for the better.

# The Conclusion Eludes Me

I have had a telescope of one kind or another for many years. A couple of years ago at Christmas my wife and her family got together to buy me a new, better, and much larger telescope than I had ever had before. I added a laser sight to it and a new world in the sky opened up to me. I began to see more and further than I had ever seen before. For me, it is too easy to dwell on the problems in my life, too easy to stress the little things. However, one look into the Orion Nebulae or out to Pleiades helps me to understand how very small and unimportant some of life's challenges can be. The universe is so large compared to the war in my head. So vast compared to my comprehension of a single intellection. It makes life as an earthling seem truly insignificant. Yet, it is all we have.

I am ever mindful of the contributions I have tried to make in life as well as my failures and triumphs, good decisions and bad, all part of the final equation. Yet it is truly impossible to conclude a story that continues and will continue, I hope, for many years to come. I have a friend who always says "I'd rather be lucky than good", a reference to the acceptance of fate over the reward of hard, thoughtful work. Sometimes it is better to cast off the chains of identity and purpose and just live and be happy. Be lucky if that is your fate, and be happy for it. I often have concluded that my purpose in this life may simply be to get some rest and be creative when it moves me. I hope to be lucky some day. I have tried so hard to be good. I know now all is not lost in a painful past. Either way the process to recover from an unpredictable violent past is a hard and painful one. Even when I am feeling good my past can haunt me like my own shadow on a sunny day.

I think I should misplace my past. Not forget or lose it anywhere. Just leave it somewhere to find another day. When I am in another space and another time it will look different. It will be different. In the mean time I will concentrate on the new things that expand my life. My telescope and rediscovered fascination with astronomy, my writing, my marriage and my new future not spent on debts from the past; the debts of regret and contempt.

Finding a star that had been lost I make my wish. My wish is to build on the dreams that had been forgotten and to always carry the hope that has been my friend. I wish to find the good buried deep in my heart. That quality that drives me to save a baby bird and care for it until it can fly on its own. Or adopt a stray dog and honor it's blessing of friendship; to render a kind word to someone in difficulty. Most of all forgive myself and others for all things now past.

0-595-24165-4

www.ingramcontent.com/pod-product-compliance
Lightning Source LLC
Chambersburg PA
CBHW020311290526
45784CB00003B/1460